DÁIL SPATS

Mary Minihan

Published in 2005
by Maverick House Publishers,
Main Street, Dunshaughlin, Co. Meath.
www.maverickhouse.com
email: info@maverickhouse.com

ISBN 1-905379-00-5

5 4 3 2 1

The paper used in this book comes from wood pulp of managed
forests. For every tree felled, at least one tree is planted, thereby
renewing natural resources.

Printed and bound by Nørhaven Paperback, Denmark.

The moral rights of the author have been asserted.

A CIP catalogue record for this book is available from the British
Library.

ACKNOWLEDGEMENTS

Thanks to the Editor of Debates, Dr. Anne Robinson, and the Ceann Comhairle, Dr. Rory O'Hanlon.

DEDICATION

For John and Catherine Minihan.

Contents

Part Three
War

Part Four
Scandals

Part Five
Coalition Tensions

INTRODUCTION

There is a widespread perception that it has been a long time since Dáil Éireann has produced any events that would rock the foundations of a Wendy house, let alone the State. That thing called 'politics' increasingly seems to be happening outside the chamber, and so Leinster House is often dismissed as dull and irrelevant.

This book sets out to prove there's life in the old Dáil yet. It brings together the most important, passionate and witty exchanges to have taken place during the Ahern administrations. Covering the years 1997 to 2005, it provides a snapshot of Irish life at a time when the State was changing rapidly.

It's little wonder that a negative view of the national parliament has arisen. Long-serving deputies have watched decision making and policy formation shift away from their Kildare Street workplace towards the social partners who meet the top tier of Government in Dublin Castle. Perhaps some of them have become despondent about their role in public life. Maybe some have stopped trying in the face of strict Dáil procedures or are frustrated with the balance of power in the House after the last election. Certainly the chamber is sadly stocked with TDs lacking the nerve to vote with their consciences against their various party lines.

TDs' 'holidays' are so good that the credibility of our politicians is further damaged every time the Dáil goes into recess. Media coverage of parliamentary proceedings is diminishing. The snappy soundbite now takes precedence over the lengthy Dáil speech. Important strategies and initiatives are launched with more fanfare elsewhere.

Then there is the gross over-dependency on scripts. All too often visitors to the public gallery nowadays hear an unenthusiastic deputy reading a cliché-heavy script produced by spin doctors and press officers. And this is frequently happening in a practically empty chamber. Assurances that other deputies are watching on monitors in their offices offer little comfort.

It is often said that great debates have become a thing of the past because all the big battles have been fought. But this is a depressing view. On occasions when the rhetoric is abandoned the results can be powerful. When this occurs we remember that what happens in Leinster House is serious and what is said there must be taken seriously.

Events can occasionally be colourful. There is parliamentary protocol, of course, and certain words are out-of-bounds. The strict rules mean TDs often get creative with their insults. Surely only in Dáil Éireann would you hear a man like Dermot Ahern use a word as quaint as 'poppycock'—not exactly common currency in his Louth constituency.

The extracts reproduced here, which come from the Official Report of the Houses of the Oireachtas and begin in the middle of the action, show Dáil Éireann in all its bizarre glory.

Mary Minihan
August 2005

PART ONE

Humour

COME IN ALBERT!

Deputy Reynolds is urged to phone home

Concern was mounting over the Dáil attendance of former Taoiseach Albert Reynolds at the end of 1997. He rejected claims that he wasn't responding to demands to turn up for votes in the chamber. But with the Government relying on the votes of Independents, things were getting tense. Pat Rabbitte (then a Democratic Left member) asked Taoiseach Bertie Ahern how efforts to locate the deputy were progressing.

(19 November 1997)

MR. [PAT] RABBITTE:	...Does the Taoiseach have knowledge of the whereabouts of Deputy Albert Reynolds? Is the Government making reasonable efforts to find him?
AN CEANN COMHAIRLE [SÉAMUS PATTISON]:	The whereabouts of any Deputy is not a matter for the Order of Business.
	(Interruptions.)
MR. RABBITTE:	On behalf of Members on this side of

the House I ask Deputy Reynolds, if he is out there, to 'phone home'.

DEMOCRATIC LEFTOVERS

And the poor old 'drunks and insomniacs'

Even Dáil deputies get that giddy end-of-term feeling. Normal hostilities were suspended as the House prepared for the long summer recess in 1998. There was movement towards a merger between Democratic Left and Labour at the time and Pat Rabbitte found himself the butt of a few jibes. In this extract, Independent Socialist TD Joe Higgins refers to the fact that Mr. Rabbitte once famously claimed that RTÉs choice of an extremely late-night slot for *Oireachtas Report* meant the programme was suitable only for 'drunks and insomniacs'.

(Elected to the Dáil as a Workers Party TD in 1989, Mr. Rabbitte left in 1992 for New Agenda. New Agenda soon changed its name to Democratic Left. Democratic Left merged with the Labour Party in 1999 and Mr. Rabbitte took the leadership in 2002.)

(03 July 1998)

MR. [PAT] RABBITTE: It goes without saying we will do everything in our power to help the Government struggle on during the summer recess.

MR. [DERMOT] AHERN: Yes, the Deputy and Vincent Browne will do so.

(Interruptions.)

AN CEANN COMHAIRLE [SÉAMUS PATTISON]: Order, please. Deputy Rabbitte should be allowed to continue.

MR. RABBITTE: Given that the worst could happen and that the Government could fall apart, will the Taoiseach indicate if the legislation on the redrawing of constituencies has been signed into law? Deputy Jim Mitchell and I would like to know where we stand.

(Interruptions.)

MR. RABBITTE: We are glad the Taoiseach and the Tánaiste will benefit from the redrawing of the constituencies. Deputy Mitchell stated yesterday that he is again considering retirement. On each occasion he does so, a general election follows six months later.

THE TAOISEACH [BERTIE AHERN]:	I thank the Ceann Comhairle and Members for their work during the session. I also thank Deputy Rabbitte for expressing his concern about the Government and I hope his party does not decide to change its name again. I know Members will be obliged to attend committee meetings for the remainder of the month but, as this is the last occasion on which the House will sit until September, I take the opportunity to state that I hope everyone will enjoy their well deserved summer break.
MR. [BRIAN] COWEN:	If Deputy Rabbitte's party changes its name again it will become known as the 'Democratic Leftovers'.
MR. [JOHN] BRUTON:	If Deputy Cowen is not careful he will be left out.
MR. [JOE] HIGGINS:	In proposing a three month break from plenary sessions of the Dáil, did the Taoiseach consider Deputy Rabbitte's 'drunks and insomniacs' who will suffer major withdrawal symptoms when 'Oireachtas Report' takes its summer break?

ANSBACHER MAN

'It is time these people were exposed'

Speculation about the identities of the Ansbacher account-holders came to a head in September 1999. A confidential list contained the names of depositors alleged to have avoided tax liability when their money was moved to the Cayman Islands. The Government was under pressure to reveal the names in the document, compiled by the Tánaiste's authorised officer, Gerard Ryan. The then Fine Gael leader, John Bruton, demanded publication, criticising what he called 'continued selective and malevolent leaking' to the media.

During this debate, Independent Socialist TD Joe Higgins offered his witty account of a day in the life of the new anti-hero of modern Irish life: Ansbacher Man. He suggested the day might kick-off with a meeting with Des Traynor (a former accountant to Charles J. Haughey) who oversaw the Ansbacher scheme.

(30 September 1999)

MR. [JOE] HIGGINS: . . . If I had time I would write a chronicle called 'A day in the life of Ansbacher Man' which would involve breakfast with Des Traynor where one would discuss the Ansbacher account and getting a loan which could be written off against one's taxes. This might be followed by morning coffee with the bank manager to discuss a few bogus non-resident accounts— Ansbacher Man being prudent not to keep all the golden eggs in one basket, that is if Ansbacher Man was not a director of the bank himself and had all the information to hand. Ansbacher Man may then be a guest speaker at a prestigious business lunch attended by the Minister for Finance where he would dwell on two themes, namely, the need to drastically cut public spending and the absolute requirement for workers' wages to be held down.

The Minister of Finance would probably flatter Ansbacher Man with an eye to the generous political contribution he hopes his political party will get on foot of an obsequious letter sent by his general secretary to Ansbacher Man and his firm. Ansbacher Man would wheel and deal perhaps in the afternoon and may then head to the Bahamas for the weekend where he would join some of his other Irish millionaire friends who do not spend as much time in Ireland because their sense of patriotism is such that they are tax exiles from the country.

No doubt their conversation would revolve around the forthcoming national wage agreement and the absolute priority of hammering wages down to the very minimum and increasing productivity. The system is rotten to the core and it is time these people were exposed.

ORGANIC LETTUCE

Serving suggestions for the Government jet

As the Ahern administration prepared to take over the EU presidency in 2004, attention turned to the need for a new Government jet to transport ministers to meetings throughout Europe. Fine Gael leader Enda Kenny wanted to know if it would be an economic model or a 'super-duper' one. The Green Party's John Gormley criticised the coalition for spending lavishly on 'chocolates and champagne'.

The Taoiseach claimed he'd never seen champagne on the jet and revealed that he didn't even eat chocolate. When Mary Coughlan, the then Social and Family Affairs Minister, observed that serving organic lettuce and brown bread might suit the Greens, Mr. Ahern said he would suggest it to the Air Corps.

(The €8 million Learjet 45 was unveiled a month after this debate took place.)

(25 November 2003)

MR. [JOHN] GORMLEY:

I was contacted by a constituent yesterday whose aunt had spent five days not on a trolley but in a Buxton chair in the Mater Hospital. How does the Taoiseach think that person feels about spending €100,000 on food, wine and luxury chocolates for the jet?

AN CEANN COMHAIRLE [RORY O'HANLON]:

That matter does not arise out of this question.

MR. GORMLEY:

Is that not an indulgence and does it not send out the wrong message to people who have to suffer cutbacks?

AN CEANN COMHAIRLE:

That issue does not arise now. The Deputy should submit a question on the matter.

MR. GORMLEY:

It arises in the context of the amount of money spent on the jet and how we use it. I would like an answer from the Taoiseach.

AN CEANN COMHAIRLE:

The Deputy has made his point.

THE TAOISEACH [BERTIE AHERN]:

Food is served on the jet. We could choose not to serve food but that would not—

Mr. Gormley:	I cannot hear the Taoiseach.
The Taoiseach:	Is the Deputy suggesting we should not serve food on the jet?
Mr. Gormley:	No, but luxury chocolates are an obscenity.
Ms. [Mary] Coughlan:	We could serve organic lettuce and brown bread.
Mr. Gormley:	People might prefer that.
An Ceann Comhairle:	Deputy Gormley, please allow the Taoiseach to continue without interruption.
The Taoiseach:	I will suggest to the Air Corps that we have organic lettuce.
	[Other questions about Ministerial transport followed but Mr. Gormley returned to his theme.]
Mr. Gormley:	In reply to my question, the Taoiseach rather flippantly said that staff would serve organic lettuce on the plane.
An Ceann Comhairle:	I am sorry, Deputy, that does not arise.
Mr. Gormley:	My question is supplementary to what the Taoiseach said. Will the

Taoiseach outline how much he has spent on food, particularly on indulgences such as chocolates and champagne?

MR. [ENDA] KENNY: Bullseyes.

MR. [SÉAMUS] BRENNAN: After Eights.

THE TAOISEACH: I have no idea how much has been spent on chocolates or champagne. I have never seen champagne on the Government jet. I will check it out but I do not think there is any.

MR. [TOM] KITT: There are no chocolates either.

THE TAOISEACH: I do not eat chocolates.

MR. GORMLEY: Someone is eating them.

MR. [JOE] HIGGINS: The pilots have scoffed them all.

As Rare as a Corncrake

A questioning Fianna Fáil backbencher pipes up

Government backbenchers are often derided for their willingness to vote along party lines, sometimes apparently against their consciences. But Independent Socialist TD Joe Higgins thought he detected signs of original thought among the compliant ranks in November 2003. His proof? Fianna Fáil deputy Jim Glennon had tabled a question to his boss, Taoiseach Bertie Ahern, on the mounting cost to the State of the Moriarty Tribunal.

(25 November 2003)

Mr. [Joe] Higgins:	The lead question is one from a Fianna Fáil backbencher—something as rare as the cry of the corncrake on a summer evening.
An Ceann Comhairle [Rory O'Hanlon]:	Has the Deputy a question?
Mr. J. Higgins:	Just when we thought questioning

Fianna Fáil backbenchers were extinct, one has croaked up, for whatever reason.

HE KNEW NOTHING

McCreevy denies that 'Parlon delivers'

On Budget Day 2003, the then Finance Minister Charlie McCreevy made the surprise announcement that 10,300 civil servants would be decentralised from Dublin. Just hours later Junior Finance Minister Tom Parlon carried out a controversial leaflet drop in the constituency he shared with the then Minister for Foreign Affairs, Brian Cowen. The fliers boasted that Mr. Parlon had delivered 965 jobs to Laois-Offaly.

In the Dáil, Mr. McCreevy eventually responded to Opposition jibes by effectively rubbishing Mr. Parlon's claim. The Minister denied his junior knew anything about the plan. As Mr. Parlon sat quietly beside him, he suggested the Minister of State had picked up the information in a pub near Leinster House the night before the Budget. In the end, Mr. McCreevy put the whole thing down to 'creative tensions', or turf wars, between Fianna Fáil and the PDs in the Laois-Offaly constituency.

(10 December 2003)

MR. [CHARLIE] McCREEVY:	. . . A question was raised yesterday about a conflict of interest in terms of Deputy Parlon and the code of conduct. The Minister of State could not possibly have breached the code of conduct as he had no hand, act or part in the process of decision making on decentralisation.

(Interruptions.)

MR. [BERNARD] DURKAN:	Deputy Parlon is on his own now. The Minister is trying to claim credit for his work.
MR. [PAUL] McGRATH:	He is getting the back of the hand.
MR. DURKAN:	Is he totally innocent?
AN LEAS-CHEANN COMHAIRLE [SÉAMUS PATTISON]:	Order, order.
MR. McCREEVY:	I regard what has gone on in the constituency of Laois–Offaly as a release of the creative tensions resulting from the stresses of multi-seat constituency politics. Deputy Parlon could not have broken the code as no Minister of State knew anything about decentralisation good, bad or indifferent.

MS. [JOAN] BURTON: Was the Minister of State lying to his constituents when he said he had delivered decentralisation?

MR. DURKAN: He was only a mascot.

MR. MCCREEVY: He made representations.

MR. DURKAN: He was totally innocent. He had nothing to do with it.

MR. MCCREEVY: Deputy Parlon had nothing to do with the decision.

MR. DURKAN: Why is he there? He is useless.

MR. MCCREEVY: I understand from sources close to Leinster House that on the Tuesday night before the budget was announced, Deputy Parlon happened to fall into certain company in a hostelry not far from here. Someone cottoned on to the fact that something might happen with decentralisation the next day. That was the extent of the Minister of State's knowledge.

MR. [CAOIMHGHÍN] Ó CAOLÁIN: I have never seen the Minister so adrift.

MR. MCCREEVY: I say the best of luck to the Minister of State. If all Deputies were up as early in the morning, Fianna Fáil would have 98 seats at every general election.

(Interruptions.)

MR. MCCREEVY:

As far as the process was concerned, Deputy Parlon was not involved. He was not involved in the decision making or the preparation. He knew nothing about it and he was as wise as everybody else. He was quicker off the blocks than everybody else. That is the truth of the matter.

(Interruptions.)

AN LEAS-CHEANN COMHAIRLE:

Order, please.

YELLOW TROUSERS

The 'Drumcondra Hare' shrugs off sartorial criticism

Following a poor result for Fianna Fáil in the 2004 local and European elections, Sinn Féin's Caoimhghín Ó Caoláin demanded to know if Taoiseach Bertie Ahern would lead the Soldiers of Destiny into the next general election. There had been speculation that Mr. Ahern might become President of the European Commission. But Mr. Ó Caoláin speculated that an 'exit strategy' to Europe wasn't on offer. 'Assuredly if it were, he would be through it as an escape hole as quick as any Drumcondra hare ever could,' the Sinn Féin deputy told the Dáil.

The Taoiseach nonchalantly insisted the job could have been his if he'd wanted it—which he didn't. And he denied that his chances were scuppered by his notorious decision to wear yellow trousers at the G8 summit in Savannah, Georgia. (Mr. Ahern's choice of a light-coloured casual outfit contrasted with the formal dark suits worn by other leaders.)

(16 June 2004)

The Taoiseach [Bertie Ahern]:	. . . In regard to the job in Europe, I think that if I were really interested in that job I would have that job.
Mr. [Bernard] Durkan:	There is confidence for you.
Mr. [Caoimhghín] Ó Caoláin:	We all believe you.
The Taoiseach:	However, when it comes to getting €1 million for working in Europe or staying at home to do the job I like doing, I will continue to do this job.
Mr. Durkan:	We really appreciate that.
Mr. [Pat] Rabbitte:	When Schröder saw the gear in Savannah, that is what did it. The Taoiseach had it up to then. He had it in the bag.
The Taoiseach:	He liked it. I had to add some colour.
Mr. Durkan:	It was the yellow trousers that did it.

'THE COUNTRY IS SAFE'

Willie O'Dea gets Defence Portfolio

Many times a Junior Minister, Willie O'Dea was risking a reputation as a political bridesmaid by 2004. He made no secret about his disappointment at being passed over for a senior post in the 2002 reshuffle. But two years later, the Limerick man finally got his feet under the Cabinet table. Over 22 years after he was first elected to the Dáil he was rewarded with the Defence portfolio—prompting Fine Gael leader Enda Kenny to salute 'Corporal O'Dea'.

(29 September 2004)

THE TAOISEACH [BERTIE AHERN]: . . . I wish to advise the House that I intend to make the following proposed reassignments. I propose to assign responsibility for the Department of Health and Children to the Tánaiste, Deputy Harney, the Department of Finance to Deputy Cowen, the Department of Communications, Marine and Natural Resources to Deputy Noel

Dempsey, the Department of Foreign Affairs to Deputy Dermot Ahern, the Department of Enterprise, Trade and Employment to Deputy Martin, the Department of Social and Family Affairs to Deputy Brennan, the Department of Transport to Deputy Cullen, the Department of Agriculture and Food to Deputy Coughlan, the Department of Education and Science to Deputy Hanafin, the Department of Defence to Deputy O'Dea—

MR. [PAUL] CONNAUGHTON:

The country is safe.

(Interruptions.)

THE TAOISEACH:

I am glad that even the Opposition agrees.

COMMIE RESISTANCE

Joe Higgins rejects the Taoiseach's socialist stance

The Taoiseach Bertie Ahern's description of himself as one of the few socialists left in Irish politics in a weekend interview with *The Irish Times* (13 November 2004) was greeted with joyful outrage by the Opposition when the Dáil resumed the following week. Labour leader Pat Rabbitte's indignation—and delight—was unbounded. He greeted 'Comrade Taoiseach' and claimed 'nothing had stretched credulity so much since the press conferences in Baghdad of "comical Ali"'.

Many noted the absence of the Dáil's only Independent Socialist TD. But Joe Higgins had been following events closely. On his return to the chamber the following day he set the Taoiseach a test to determine whether or not the 'conversion' was genuine. According to Deputy Higgins, Mr. Ahern 'flunked'.

(17 November 2004)

MR. [JOE] HIGGINS: Many of today's newspapers were kind enough to point out that I was not in the House yesterday when the Labour Party leader asked the Taoiseach about his new found commitment to socialism. Ironically, I was abroad for several days on political work to advance the cause of socialism.

MR. [PAT] RABBITTE: Did the Deputy have the Government jet?

(Interruptions.)

MR. J. HIGGINS: You can imagine, a Cheann Comhairle, how perplexed I was when I returned to find my wardrobe almost empty. The Taoiseach had been busy robbing my clothes. Up to recently the Progressive Democrats did not have a stitch left due to the same Taoiseach but we never expected him to take a walk on the left side of the street.

THE TAOISEACH [BERTIE AHERN]:   Extreme left.

MR. J. HIGGINS: He said, 'I am one of the few socialists left in Irish politics'. Immediately, Tomás Ó Criomhthaín came to mind, as he lamented the last of the Blasket Islanders.
'Ní bheidh ár leithéidí arís ann.'

I then thought, 'Good, Taoiseach. There are two of us in it and we will go down together.'

Sadly, I had to take a reality check. If this conversion was genuine we would have to go back 2,000 years to find another as rapid and as radical. Saul's embrace of Christianity on the road to Damascus stood the test of time but the Taoiseach's embrace of socialism on the banks of the Tolka hardly will.

I was not impressed with the Taoiseach's answers yesterday so I will set him a test on three brief points to check if he is a socialist. On public ownership, the Taoiseach stated—

THE TAOISEACH: Is the Deputy inquiring if I am a positive or a negative socialist? He is a socialist of the negative kind.

MR. J. HIGGINS: We will see if the Taoiseach answers in the positive. Public ownership is crucial for socialists and the Taoiseach stated that he likes the idea that the Phoenix Park and the Botanic Gardens are publicly owned. As has been stated, however, he gave our telecommunications industry to venture capitalists to play around with. Will the Taoiseach answer the question to which he failed to reply just now? The Government is split on Aer Lingus and the Minister for Justice, Equality and Law Reform, Deputy McDowell, wants it to be in private hands. Will the Taoiseach—?

AN CEANN COMHAIRLE [RORY O'HANLON]:

The Chair is reluctant to intervene but the Deputy's time is concluded.

MR. J. HIGGINS:

The second test is that democratic socialists never support imperialist invasions and certainly those of the type launched by the US military which is wading in blood through Fallujah. The Taoiseach helped the US military to get there. Will he now denounce that atrocity, and condemn the murder of an innocent Iraqi as we this morning condemned those obscurantists who murder innocent hostages?

On equality, the Taoiseach stated that he is happy that the children in Rutland Street school are given breakfast there. Why should they be obliged to depend on the school for their breakfast? It is because he has presided over one of the most unequal regimes in the western world which has given huge concessions to big business while poverty remains in our State.

The Taoiseach has three minutes in which to reply. I suggest that he devote one minute to each of the three tests and I will judge his replies at the end.

THE TAOISEACH: I would never consider that I subscribe to the same kind of politics or ideology as Deputy Joe Higgins.

MR. [MICHAEL D.] HIGGINS: The Taoiseach has scored a 'D' grade already.

THE TAOISEACH: My politics and ideology might be closer to those of Deputy Michael D. Higgins. I have watched and listened to Deputy Joe Higgins with interest for three decades but I have never heard him say anything positive. He displays what I believe to be a far left or 'commie' resistance to everything. He does so in the hope that some day the world will discover oil wells off our coast which will fall into the ownership of the State, thereby allowing us to run a great market economy with the State at its centre. That utopia does not exist.

What I said yesterday when the Deputy was not present is that—

MR. J. HIGGINS: I read what the Taoiseach said yesterday. He should just answer the questions I have put to him now.

THE TAOISEACH: —at the core of left centre political ideology is the desire to spread the wealth more evenly. That means that people must be encouraged to create the wealth. When this is done, they are taxed and the money collected, is used to resource them.

(Interruptions.)

AN CEANN COMHAIRLE: Deputies should allow the Taoiseach to continue, without interruption.

THE TAOISEACH: Deputy Joe Higgins is against wealth creation and, as a result, he favours high unemployment, high expenditure and high borrowing. Any of the tests the Deputy would set me fail on the grounds that he does not believe in them. That is the issue. What we do is create the wealth, thereby allowing ourselves to employ 100,000 people in the health services to care for others, tens of thousands of teachers, many community care professionals and resource and home liaison teachers and teachers to look after the disadvantaged in our schools.

That is what our brand of socialism allows us to do. The Deputy's brand of socialism has changed so much in recent years. As he is aware, one of the reasons for the rise in oil prices is because his friends in Russia have decided that the market economy can afford $50 a barrel.

(Interruptions.)

DR. [JERRY] COWLEY: We had oil wells off the coast and the Taoiseach gave them away.

THE TAOISEACH: The Deputy is a right-wing doctor.

MR. [DERMOT] AHERN: And a well paid one.

THE TAOISEACH: That is what is wrong with Deputy Joe Higgins's policies. I would be delighted to discuss the matter with him on the Blaskets or elsewhere whenever he likes.

THE NON-RESIDENT STALLION

'Does the Cinderella rule apply?'

Any casual observer of Irish politics knows about non-resident accounts. But what about non-resident stallions? In this straight-faced debate with Finance Minister Brian Cowen, Labour's Joan Burton wanted to know if members of the bloodstock industry trotted out of the country before midnight on a particular date, could their owners avail of a generous tax break.

(01 February 2005)

Ms. [JOAN] BURTON: Stallions can be non-resident for six months a year with their owners still benefitting from the tax break. This tax break is in place at a time when pensioners pay tax on modest incomes. Are there tests of what constitutes six months non-residence for stallions? In particular, does the Cinderella rule apply? For example, if a stallion is out of the country before midnight, does that count as a full day?

MR. COWEN:	I am taken by the obsession of the Labour Party with the stallion.
MR. [FINIAN] MCGRATH:	Has the Minister tips for tomorrow's races?
MR. COWEN:	Indecon, which is regarded a reputable team of consultants, independently compiled a report on behalf of the Irish Thoroughbred Breeders' Association and Horse Racing Ireland. Indecon estimates the gross figure foregone is €3 million, although I do not say I agree. I will find out about the Cinderella clause, about which the Deputy is worried, and whether a stallion must be out of the country before or after midnight. That does not make much sense but I will inquire into it.
MS. BURTON:	It is important for non-resident taxpayers.
MR. COWEN:	I did not know they had to be accompanied by a stallion.

PART TWO

Harsh Words

THE 'BOY' MINISTER AND THE 'HALF-BOY' MINISTER FOR STATE

Quinn takes on Martin and O'Dea

Labour's Rúairí Quinn took a swipe at the experientially-challenged Micheál Martin and the vertically-restricted Willie O'Dea in November 1998, when they were Education Minister and Junior Education Minister respectively. The Labour Party had initiated a debate on student poverty and the accommodation crisis. Mr. Quinn challenged the 'young, strident and ambitious' Mr. Martin to 'come clean' on where he stood on university fees.

Earlier, after a string of Fianna Fáil backbenchers had spoken almost adoringly of Mr. Martin, Michael D. Higgins mused that nobody in Irish history had been praised more, 'except perhaps Daniel O'Connell, although even he had an occasional detractor.' Warming to his theme, he continued, 'It is said that people faint at the sound of the Minister's name in every part of the country.'

(25 November 1998)

MR. [RÚAIRÍ] QUINN:	It is with some sadness that I rise to speak on behalf of my party, and I welcome the support of Democratic Left and Fine Gael. If Donogh O'Malley, a former Fianna Fáil Deputy for Limerick, the constituency the Minister of State represents, adopted the philosophy which has just been enunciated, he would never have introduced the universal abolition of second level fees.
MR. [WILLIE] O'DEA:	That is simply not true.
MR. QUINN:	The Minister has missed the point, but that does not surprise me. Fianna Fáil is now talking about targeting and selectivity, a complete repudiation of the principle of universality which the British Government applied to primary education, which Donogh O'Malley, an icon of the Fianna Fáil Party, introduced in relation to second level and which we unashamedly introduced at third level. ·
MR. [MICHEÁL] MARTIN:	You did not.
MR. QUINN:	We did. We abolished fees.
MR. MARTIN:	The second level reforms were about places. The Government of which the

Deputy was a member did not create one additional place.

MR. QUINN: We abolished fees. If the boy Minister and the half boy Minister of State wish to interrupt me then I will engage them. Access to education concerns a principle and a value, something Fianna Fáil may have difficulty in understanding. It is not just about places or the number of classrooms, but the right to be in whatever places exist irrespective of family income. It is about the right to be there irrespective of income.

MR. MARTIN: If there is a place.

MR. QUINN: We are not talking about some half baked aristocracy, but about the right of every citizen to be there if they qualify. It is then one can talk about the availability of places. When we introduced the abolition of fees in third level we were addressing a principle and a value which Fianna Fáil, through Donogh O'Malley, addressed wonderfully in the 1960s. The well-to-do middle classes were ripping off the tax system through tax covenants. Tax covenants of the order of £3 million from the turn of the century had applied to a small category of people. In 1993–4, when we were in Government with Fianna Fáil, we noticed a sudden escalation in the tax foregone on covenants which rose exponentially from between £3 million and £4 million to £38 million. In middle class suburbs in my constituency and elsewhere there were back to back covenants, where the 5 per cent did not apply. Who was able to apply?

The answer is the fat cats and the rich people who had the income to write unlimited cheques for their neighbours and their neighbours' children, while the people who lost out were the children of creamery workers and others who barely qualified for a grant or who were £3 or £4 over the threshold on the basis of PAYE.

We killed two things with the one stone, namely, the denial of the principle of universal access in relation to fees, perhaps the last country in the EU to do so. Greece, Portugal and Spain, which are poorer than Ireland, had no university fees for those who qualified for entry. We were the last country in the EU to get rid of fees. We also closed a middle class tax loophole for which I make no apology.

I challenge the young, strident and ambitious Minister for Education and Science—good luck to him—to come clean on where he stands on university fees. Is he in favour of their reintroduction? That is not clear. If equity means anything then grants should be assessed on the net income of a household. There has been a scandal in the past—

MR. MARTIN: The Deputy was Minister for Finance for three years.

MR. QUINN: I did not have £1,000 million to bank.

MR. MARTIN: The Deputy should have abolished tax covenants.

AN CEANN COMHAIRLE [SÉAMUS PATTISON]: There should be no further interruptions.

MR. QUINN: The truth hurts. When one is as ambitious as the Minister for Education and Science the truth hurts very much.

MR. MARTIN: I am not at all ambitious.

MR. QUINN: We heard the Minister's disclaimers. The Taoiseach should walk with his back close to the wall.

MR. MARTIN:	Many people in the Deputy's party should walk with their backs to the wall.
MR. QUINN:	Who? Will the Minister permit me to make a speech? This is a debating Chamber and I am addressing the points which have been made.
MR. MARTIN:	The Deputy can give it but he cannot take it.
MR. QUINN:	I will take anything the Minister wishes to give. What does he wish to say to me?
AN CEANN COMHAIRLE:	There should be no interruptions.
MR. MARTIN:	The Deputy was Minister for Finance for three years and did not address the issue.
MR. QUINN:	That is not true. In the three budgets I introduced, in the time available to me and given the background which existed, we did more than was previously done in relation to third level education. The abolition of fees was the first phase. We also made provision for capital infrastructural investment in third level education and we went on to do more. However,

I am not here to argue my record but rather to talk about what can be done now against a background of a surplus of £1,000 million.

I wish to talk about accommodation. I understand the young Minister for Education and Science, who is filled with the wisdom of 17 months in office, accused me of making a declaration of commitment off the back of a lorry. There was a debate in my parliamentary party and we agreed the motion in the name of all members of the parliamentary party which was deferred to take account of an all-party Opposition motion relating to a health issue. We contacted people with whom we were in discussion to inform them of this development. This is not some recent conversion. My commitment to student politics and rights goes back some time, I suspect a little longer than the Minister's.

MR. [PAT] RABBITTE: The Minister was in the cradle.

This 'Tacky' Motion

Beverley Cooper-Flynn stands by her dad

Having told Taoiseach Bertie Ahern that 'a Flynn must support a Flynn', the EU Commissioner's daughter took a dramatic decision to vote against the Government in February 1999. At issue was the allegation that £50,000 intended for, but never passed to Fianna Fáil, had been given to Pádraig Flynn when he was Environment Minister by property developer Tom Gilmartin. Mr. Flynn refused to comment on the controversy. He insisted the appropriate forum into planning matters and payments was the Flood Tribunal (where he eventually took the stand in 2004).

The Opposition demanded the Dáil consider whether it was of the opinion that Mr. Flynn should continue as Commissioner if he did not respond to the charge, notwithstanding the ongoing work of the tribunal. The Government's amendment to the Opposition motion stressed the importance of allowing the tribunal to complete its work. But it did call for Mr. Flynn to clarify his position immediately. In response, Ms. Cooper-Flynn said that she could not believe Fianna Fáil would 'collaborate' with the Opposition parties on such a 'tacky' motion.

(10 February 1999)

Ms. [BEVERLEY] COOPER-FLYNN:

Fine Gael has knowingly wasted the time of this House on something which can and will have no effect on the man it is setting out to damage. Although it will have no effect on the Commissioner, it will have a negative effect elsewhere. If there is anything calculated to increase public cynicism about politics, it is watching the second largest party in Dáil Éireann knowingly wasting parliamentary time on something pointless. It sends an interesting message about how Fine Gael views the business of Opposition—never mind the reality, feel the headlines. It is bad enough to engage in a pointless and fruitless form of games playing, but it is much worse to do it in such a tacky way.

The Fine Gael recipe is as follows: throw together a motion, lash in a couple of 'notwithstandings', stir in a bit of guilt by association and maybe it will look as if it benefits somebody. This motion will not benefit anybody. It is filled with the pretence that it is all straightforward and that if one has nothing to hide, one can make an immediate statement. However, it is not straightforward. If it was, we would not have had all the argument in the Flood Tribunal about who gives what evidence first, who gets to cross-examine whom and who might lose out by not having vital information other people have.

The people who crafted this motion are asking the European Commissioner not only to bypass a tribunal set up by this House and to risk condemnation by Mr. Justice Flood, but to behave as only a naive fool would behave. If two people's accounts of an event differ, then to ask one of those people to sacrifice due process, to lay all his evidence on the table and to present his entire case before he gets near the tribunal is to effectively sacrifice one party in an argument to the interests of the other. That is not justice.

Man's capacity for justice, it has been said, makes democracy possible, but man's inclination to injustice makes democracy necessary. We, for all our faults and failings, are the trusted guardians of democracy. By setting up the Flood Tribunal, this House, by unanimous consent, honoured its duty to the principles of democracy.

Tonight we are attempting to subvert the structure we set up and to pre-empt the findings and deliberations of that body. If this was a rush to judgment, it would be reprehensible enough but it is a blatant attempt to sacrifice the good name and reputation of someone who is outside this House and whose only sin is to offer to abide by the procedures we have set up and demanded obedience to, namely the Flood Tribunal.

This motion is a fake in every way. It pretends to be concerned about an allegation that appeared in print five months ago. It was made public almost half a year ago. What is new to justify the hysterical tone of this motion? What is different? Did new information emerge? All we have is a restatement of an untried allegation. The man making this untried allegation has restated that he did not ask the former Minister for the Environment for a favour nor did he receive one. That is precisely the position we were at five months ago. Hence we have the extraordinary frenzy of a fortnight ago when the Tánaiste announced that the Commissioner's position was now 'impossible'. That is clearly not true. Jacques Santer does not think his position is impossible and the

Government knows his position is not impossible.

People tend to keep doing things for which they are rewarded. Fianna Fáil should not collude in its own destruction or in the continuing portrayal of our party as intrinsically, essentially and eternally flawed by seeming to reward others who claim to be our moral guardians. Every time we do it, we are buying today's survival at the cost of tomorrow's existence. We are eroding our faith in ourselves and we are betraying our supporters.

When today's proceedings are over, I urge that all Members of the House stand back and reflect on what has been happening over the past three months. We have seen the work of the Oireachtas trivialised and we have nobody to blame but ourselves. We set up tribunals and then we run scared, unwilling and unable to wait on the due process they entail. We are the elected representatives of the people, yet we allow ourselves to become putty in the hands of influences around and outside us.

That is why, until I see the votes counted, I will not bring myself to believe that the party I know would collaborate with the Opposition parties on this tacky motion. The Fianna Fáil Party which I believe has a future, would not collaborate with the Opposition in its attempt to damage a man Fianna Fáil knows is committed to Ireland in Europe in a powerfully effective way. The Fianna Fáil Party, which should lead this country in the next century, would not abandon leadership on this issue and it would not act as if it was helpless in the face of an unstoppable process.

Above all, it would not ask its members to put their names to something which, as individuals, they neither believe in nor approve. In loyalty to the Fianna Fáil Party, its ideals, leadership and members who have shown me such friendship and support, not least in the past few days, I will not put my name to a motion which is empty except for the seeds of the long-term damage to my party.

'The Taoiseach Should
Stick to his Script'

Bertie Ahern denies Fianna Fáil benefited from the passports-for-sale scheme

In February 1999, *The Irish Times* reported that money was diverted from a passport investor's ICC bank account to a Fianna Fáil account six years earlier (when the Taoiseach Bertie Ahern had been party treasurer). It was also reported that former Foreign Affairs Minister Ray Burke had offered to tell the Flood Tribunal all that he knew on condition that he be granted immunity.

In the Dáil, the Taoiseach was adamant on the matter of immunity. 'It is important for me to say I have no power over immunities for people at the tribunal. A request was not made to give anyone immunity. I have no knowledge of a request for immunity. Nobody raised anything about immunities for the former Deputy, Ray Burke.'

Later he explained that the £10,500 being referred to was an interest-free loan, transferred and not diverted from an ICC deposit account to a Fianna Fáil fundraising account. 'Nothing underhand, deceitful or criminal took place in the transfer of funds.'

He subsequently revealed his frustration in ad-libbed comments during hostile exchanges prompting Fine Gael's

Ivan Yates to wryly advise him to 'stick to his script'. But Mr. Ahern concluded that the Government was 'clean on all of these issues which have been thrown at us this week.'

(18 February 1999)

MR. [DONAL] CAREY:	The Dáil does not matter.
THE TAOISEACH:	The Deputy should stay quiet.
AN LEAS-CHEANN COMHAIRLE [RORY O'HANLON]:	The Taoiseach without interruption.
THE TAOISEACH:	What is happening is that people are throwing muck and hoping that some of it sticks. There have been five issues this week and I could mention five more on which people are digging around.
MR. [IVAN] YATES:	Do not stop now.
AN LEAS-CHEANN COMHAIRLE:	The Taoiseach without interruption.
THE TAOISEACH:	I could come in armed very differently. I could bring in all the files that have gone to the tribunal because I have the records. I could say who did what during their time in office. I could go

around the House and raise issues.

MR. YATES: The Taoiseach is spending a lot of time on it.

MR. [JOHN] BRUTON: Should that be taken as a threat?

THE TAOISEACH: The Deputies should be quiet.

MR. YATES: The Tánaiste is looking decidedly uncomfortable.

AN LEAS-CHEANN COMHAIRLE: The Taoiseach without interruption.

MR. J. BRUTON: Is the Taoiseach threatening the Opposition?

THE TAOISEACH: Nobody is threatening anybody.

MR. YATES: The Taoiseach should stick to his script.

MR. J. BRUTON: It sounds like a threat, but they do not count here.

AN LEAS-CHEANN COMHAIRLE: The Taoiseach without interruption.

THE TAOISEACH: The Deputy should not lose his temper. He is quick to lose his temper. As soon as anything gets to him, he gets excited.

MR. J. BRUTON:	Will the Taoiseach yield?
THE TAOISEACH:	No.
AN LEAS-CHEANN COMHAIRLE:	The Taoiseach had said he will not yield, which is his prerogative.
MR. J. BRUTON:	The Taoiseach said he would go through the files of all the Deputies in the House.
AN LEAS-CHEANN COMHAIRLE:	The Taoiseach without interruption.
THE TAOISEACH:	If I did not hear everything on 'Morning Ireland' correctly this morning, I apologise.
MR. J. BRUTON:	Is the Taoiseach apologising?
MR. [PAT] RABBITTE:	Why did the Taoiseach not put on a spokesman?
A DEPUTY:	He did not do so out of respect for the House.
THE TAOISEACH:	Deputy Bruton misheard me. I said I could mention all the files relating to different Governments which have gone to the tribunal. That does not mean anything was wrong but I could play the innuendo game.

MR. DURKAN:	The Taoiseach is doing that anyway.
THE TAOISEACH:	I am not doing that. The files relate to periods under different Governments.
MR. J. BRUTON:	The Taoiseach should not threaten the Opposition.
THE TAOISEACH:	Nobody is threatening anybody. Who is getting threats all week?
MR. [ULICK] BURKE:	The Taoiseach should look behind him.
THE TAOISEACH:	Deputy Bruton said I was getting excited about immunity, but that he did not raise the issue. However, the Deputy's notice under Standing Order 31 mentioned an offer of immunity to someone willing to testify to the Flood tribunal.
MR. J. BRUTON:	There is no mention of the Taoiseach.
THE TAOISEACH:	What else could one read into it?.
MR. [MICHEÁL] MARTIN:	What else was it about?
MR. J. BRUTON:	It is a legitimate issue.

AN LEAS-CHEANN COMHAIRLE:

The Taoiseach without interruption.

THE TAOISEACH:

A question was asked about the diversion of money. Deputy Quinn's notice under Standing Order 31 states: The allegations made in a newspaper article that a sum of around £10,000 was diverted from the account of a passport investor to a Fianna Fáil controlled account in another financial institution in 1993 at a time when the current Taoiseach was treasurer of the Fianna Fáil Party and the need for the Taoiseach to make a full statement on the matter.

Deputy John Bruton's notice states: The admission by a Government source today that money has been accepted by Fianna Fáil from a passports for investment investor; Deputy Gormley's notice sought the adjournment of the House 'to allow time for a debate on the revelations that a transfer of £10,000 from an ICC account of a passport investor to a Fianna Fáil account in another institution took place in 1993.'

MR. J. BRUTON:

To what is the Taoiseach referring?

THE TAOISEACH:

I am outlining the questions which

were raised and trying to answer them.

MR. J. BRUTON: It sounds like the Taoiseach is reading a telephone book.

THE TAOISEACH: The Deputy appears upset.

MR. YATES: Mr. Burke has the Taoiseach upset.

MR. D. CAREY: The Taoiseach has plenty of reasons to be upset.

THE TAOISEACH: Not at all. I am enjoying myself.

MR. [CONOR] LENIHAN: Reading a telephone book is more interesting than listening to the Opposition.

New GUBU

The coalition limps over the line

The Government defeated a No Confidence motion in June 2000. But the crisis-stricken coalition just about made it to the summer recess. The trial of former Taoiseach Charlie Haughey for obstructing the McCracken Tribunal had been halted because of Tánaiste Mary Harney's comment that he should be convicted and jailed. Fianna Fáil had just taken a hammering in a by-election. And the Taoiseach Bertie Ahern was experiencing dangerous fallout from a series of, frankly unfortunate, cabinet appointments he had made.

Delivering a damning state-of-the-government address, then Fine Gael leader John Bruton claimed it was 'grotesque, at the beginning of this millennium, that we still have in office as Taoiseach someone who signed thousands of blank cheques for Charlie Haughey'. The GUBU days were back, he claimed. Events were once again 'grotesque, unbelievable, bizarre and unprecedented' (borrowing the phrase used by the former Taoiseach after the discovery of killer Malcolm MacArthur in the flat of Government Attorney General Patrick Connolly in 1982.

The acronym GUBU was subsequently coined by Conor
Cruise O'Brien.)

(30 June 2000)

MR. [JOHN] BRUTON: It is bizarre that we have a Fianna
Fáil Party still in office that could
select Ray Burke to be Foreign
Minister, Deputy Foley as its senior
representative on a Dáil committee
to maintain financial probity, Deputy
Lawlor as its representative on a Dáil
committee on political ethics and
Deputy Ellis to head a Dáil committee
to protect the financial interests of
farmers.

MR. [DERMOT] AHERN: That is ironic coming from Deputy
Bruton.

MR. J. BRUTON: It is unprecedented that we still
have a Tánaiste whose loose words
brought down the first ever criminal
trial in northern Europe of a former
Prime Minister and who has not yet
apologised for what she did to the
Dáil or to the people.

MR. [DICK] ROCHE: Does Deputy Bruton have any policies
about which he wishes to speak?

MR. J. BRUTON:

It may well be grotesque, unbelievable, bizarre and unprecedented, but none of this is accidental, nor is it unpredictable.

The core of the problem lies in the motor force of the Fianna Fáil Party. That party has elevated pragmatism to be the supreme political value. While it still retains some antique prejudices—these were displayed during earlier interruptions—

MR. ROCHE:

Pragmatism beats the hell out of total confusion.

MR. J. BRUTON:

—it has elevated pragmatism to be the supreme political virtue. There is no longer any principle for which Fianna Fáil would be willing to sacrifice office.

MR. [MARTIN] CULLEN:

That is absolute rubbish.

MR. J. BRUTON:

That ultimate pragmatism, that vacuum of political principle—

(Interruptions.)

AN CEANN COMHAIRLE [SÉAMUS PATTISON]:

Order, please.

MR. J. BRUTON: —has created an opening through which certain business interests were able to colonise and corrupt top level members of Fianna Fáil unbeknown to most of its loyal supporters throughout the country—

MR. ROCHE: Does the Deputy have any policies about which he wants to speak? Does his party have a single policy—

AN CEANN COMHAIRLE: If Deputy Roche continues to interrupt I will have to ask him to leave the House.

MR. [BRIAN] HAYES: Hear, hear.

MR. [RÚAIRÍ] QUINN: The Ceann Comhairle should leave the Deputy alone because he is only trying to obtain a promotion.

AN CEANN COMHAIRLE: Deputy Bruton, without interruption.

MR. J. BRUTON: That elevation of pragmatism as the only political value has created an opening through which people who simply want their own way or who are pursuing solely their own financial interests have been able to corrupt top level members of the Fianna Fáil Party. If Fianna Fáil had strong economic, political or social principles for which it would be willing to sacrifice office, that corruption would have been impossible. Until Fianna Fáil reinvents itself as a party, with strong and controversial beliefs with which some people disagree, it will continue to be, through an excess of pragmatism, prey to corruption by those whose only aim is to make money or get their own way.

It is time for plain speaking. This motion of no confidence in the Government is a gesture. The contrary motion of confidence which was moved this morning will be passed this afternoon. It is a sign of the extent to which modern language has been emptied of all meaning that the confidence motion in this disgraceful Government will be carried by the votes of Deputies who describe themselves as 'Independents' and by four other Deputies whose party describes itself as 'Progressive'.

DR. [MICHAEL] WOODS:	That is democracy.
MR. D. AHERN:	Remember Eoin O'Duffy.

(Interruptions.)

AN CEANN COMHAIRLE:	Deputy Bruton, without interruption.
MR. J. BRUTON:	The so-called Independents who are actually dependent on Fianna Fáil and the Progressive Democrats are slowly but surely regressing back into the Fianna Fáil Party from which they emerged.
MRS. [NORA] OWEN:	That is right, you can see the seams.
MR. J. BRUTON:	It is indeed a time for plain speaking. There is little point in voting no confidence in a Government unless you are willing and able to inform the people how and by whom you intend to replace it. Under our constitutional procedures, Fianna Fáil will remain in office, even after a general election, until it is replaced. In a general election, the people will want renewal but they will also want certainty. Independent candidates who cannot say for sure whether, by vote or abstention, they will re-elect Fianna Fáil after the election will not be providing the people with the certainty they need.

Fine Gael will not support Fianna Fáil in Government after the next election by external support, by coalition or by any other method.

(Interruptions.)

AN CEANN
COMHAIRLE:

Order, please.

MR. J. BRUTON:

Difficult as it may be for Deputies opposite to believe, I say this without antipathy towards any individual member of the Fianna Fáil Party and without lack of appreciation of the beneficial role that party has played in Irish history. I have acknowledged Fianna Fáil's contribution to this State on many occasions in the House and I will do so again.

In my opinion Fianna Fáil will renew itself. I believe it can, and probably will, again become a party of principle and a truly national movement. However, it will never do that from a base in Government Buildings. If Fianna Fáil is to renew itself, it must first be in opposition.

MR. D. AHERN:

We were in opposition prior to the last election.

MR. J. BRUTON:

The 54 Deputies for whom I speak are the ones in this House who guarantee that after the next election Fianna Fáil will be in opposition. That is the message I will be giving to the Irish people during the next three months.

Fianna Fáil will win this afternoon's vote. However, as far as I am concerned, whether it is to last two months or two years, the general election campaign will start at 5 p.m. today.

(Interruptions.)

AN CEANN COMHAIRLE:

Order, please.

MR. BRUTON:

This country needs a real Government, not 15 tribunal watchers sitting in Government Buildings with their minds on other matters.

MR. [MICHAEL] SMITH:

Sanctimonious humbug.

'Naked Anarchy'

'Fianna Fáil is afraid of taxi drivers'

The intensity of the taxi drivers' response to the deregulation of their industry took the Government by surprise. There was traffic chaos in November 2000 as drivers mounted blockades outside Leinster House, at Dublin Port and Dublin Airport, and in other cities. It was 'naked anarchy', according to Fine Gael's Jim Higgins. The then Justice Minister, John O'Donoghue, came under pressure in the Dáil to reveal what he was doing about it. He said the disruption taxi drivers were causing to their fellow citizens could not be justified. But he insisted he would not be interfering in Garda efforts to resolve the situation, which was 'one for professional police judgement'. The Opposition dismissed this as a 'classic Pontius Pilate response', with Michael Creed of Fine Gael claiming the taxi drivers had Fianna Fáil running scared.

(22 November 2000)

MR. [JIM] HIGGINS:

Notwithstanding that this is a difficult and volatile situation which the Minister seems to think is changing by the hour, does he not agree it involves naked anarchy and a complete disregard for law and public order? Why is such special consideration being given to taxi drivers? This is not an orderly protest but an illegal blockade. Would the Minister agree that if any other vested interest group mounted similar action it would be dealt with very swiftly, cars would be moved on and people would be arrested and, perhaps, have their property impounded? What action will be taken to ensure this matter is dealt with before 7 p.m. or 8 p.m.?

MR. [JOHN] O'DONOGHUE:

The Deputy understands how difficult this situation is for the Garda. It is a question of managing the situation from hour to hour. The Garda has to be pragmatic and does not wish to exacerbate the situation. It must be clear to the Deputy that it would be a mistake to do so. It is not a case of the Garda giving special consideration to any one group but of gardaí on the scene being pragmatic. It is for them to direct operational matters and I have the fullest confidence in them to do so.

MR. [RÚAIRÍ] QUINN: The Minister has given the House a classic Pontius Pilate response and it is deeply politically poignant it should come from someone who trumpeted zero tolerance as a political slogan when in Opposition. Would the Minister agree that to describe the Garda's approach to manifest law breaking on a scale of anarchy which is bringing this city to a standstill in many respects as a 'pragmatic approach' is manifest nonsense? The Minister has professional skills as an officer of the court in his capacity as a solicitor, a practice in which he is not currently engaged. However, would he agree that his knowledge would inform him that this is not a pragmatic response from the Garda?

The Garda has an obligation to enforce the law and part of that law is to maintain public order. That is not to remove the legitimate right of people who feel their contract of trust with Fianna Fáil and the Government has been unilaterally broken. Such people can protest in many ways but not necessarily at the total, utter and continued inconvenience of citizens. Will the Minister tell the House whether he will request the Garda Commissioner to ensure that the rule of law prevails, that the public highway is kept open and allow the operational implementation of that enforcement of law to be a matter of judgment for the commissioner and his senior officers in the Dublin metropolitan area?

Would the Minister further agree that his response is totally inadequate? If he was in the position he occupied for four and a half years and Deputy Owen was Minister he would be roaring from the rooftops for action on this issue. He is applying two standards to political responsibility, one in Opposition and one in Government.

MR. O'DONOGHUE: Over the past three years I have become used to being second-guessed by Deputy Quinn and other Deputies but comparisons are odious. It must be clear to the Deputy that this is not a Pontius Pilate exercise. The issue is an operational matter for the Garda. Is any Deputy seriously arguing that the Minister for Justice, Equality and Law Reform should direct the Garda to arrest a person or group of persons? I did not do so in Opposition.

Deputy Quinn rightly stated that people cannot disobey the law and those involved in demonstrations of this type are also subject to the law governing activities in public places. There is a general obligation on persons engaged in such demonstrations or protests not to wilfully obstruct traffic or to engage in any disruptive behaviour in breach of the law. Legislation governing this area includes the Road Traffic Acts, 1961 to 1995, and the Criminal Justice (Public Order) Act, 1994. No amount of argument can hide the fact that there are practical problems in this situation.

MR. QUINN: Like what?

MR. O'DONOGHUE: Like exacerbating what is a very sensitive and difficult situation on the ground.

MR. [MICHAEL] CREED: Fianna Fáil is afraid of taxi drivers.

'SNAP, CRACKLE AND POP'

Mary O'Rourke bites back

The Opposition demanded that Taoiseach Bertie Ahern sack his then Minister for Public Enterprise, Mary O'Rourke, in November 2001. Fine Gael, Labour and the Greens proposed a vote of no confidence, accusing her of bungling her dealings with State-sponsored companies. The Minister had just been photographed with a Luas tram in Dublin's Merrion Square—at least two years before the light rail system was due to open to the public (and three years before it actually was). The then Fine Gael leader Michael Noonan claimed this piece of 'toy track' was the latest political gimmick by a desperate government.

'If the Minister wants to play with toy trains, she should invest in a good set and play with them at home, or write to Santa Claus,' he said. Labour's Rúairí Quinn claimed Mrs. O'Rourke was the Taoiseach's 'patsy' and was 'sadly out of her depth'.

Mrs. O'Rourke came out fighting. The attacks prompted this vigorous response, which at times came close to slapstick. She denounced Mr. Quinn as a 'misplaced character from "Noddy Gets Narky"' who needed to learn that there was 'more to politics than turning red and making one's eyes bulge'. Recalling Mrs. O'Rourke's infamous admission that she had been bathing when she heard an important newsflash (that CIÉ chairman Brian Joyce had resigned), Labour's Emmet Stagg suggested she 'get back into her bath and cool off'.

(06 November 2001)

MRS. [MARY]
O'ROURKE:

There was an era when Private Members' time in this House was used as a vehicle to advance the Opposition's policy platform. That was when the time was used to debate Private Members' Bills or policies drafted and published by the Opposition, but that time has long gone. For Private Members' time to be used constructively it is necessary to have an Opposition with something constructive to contribute. This is not such an Opposition. It is an Opposition without courage or vision, it is indolent and led by lazy leaders. It is a soft option Opposition which is prepared to criticise the proposals of others but has no policy of its own.

Tonight the Opposition is unable to suggest solutions and engages in unfocused criticism. I do not know whether the lack of motivation and focus in Fine Gael is the result of their in-fighting and internal intrigue or disillusionment and despair, but it is palpable. If Fine Gael spent half as much time developing policies as it did soliciting and concealing offshore donations and evading tax, lazy motions like this would never see the light of day. Deputy Noonan is inert, inactive and unable. He appears to have exhausted himself in the course of the relentless whispering campaign he conducted against his former leader. For a man so active and agile while in the shadows, it is sad to see his sloth in sunlight. He was lively when he was plotting to get rid of Deputy John Bruton and sacking the old front bench.

MR. [DAVID] STANTON:

That is a personal attack; the Minister should stick to the issues.

MRS. O'ROURKE:

But when he got the job he became listless and lazy. It is a curious logic—perhaps unique to Fine Gael—that Deputy Bruton had to go because he was unpopular, but Deputy Noonan must stay because he is more unpopular. From the Government benches it is possible to see beyond Deputy Noonan. It is possible to see the cringing faces of the newly demoted—and those of the yet to be promoted—as he unleashes yet another tortured cliché. It is possible to see the wasted generations of Fine Gael who still wonder why it is 19 years since the people chose Fine Gael to lead a Government after a general election. The answer is slowly dawning—the answer is Deputy Noonan. The people have had enough of the politics of finger-pointing, the politics of carping criticism and the politics of relentless negativism. They want a Government which is united and decisive. Deputy Noonan will never lead such a Government.

The Fine Gael Leader is no more than a collection of clichés which are worn, tired and tortured. Tonight he has called for my resignation. I will be here long after those who now sit behind and whisper about Deputy Noonan have sent him off. This motion is as predictable as it is lazy. It is a product of the feet-on the-desk and the head back school of politics. It is a symptom of 'the anything will do because we're going to give the same speech anyway' approach. It comes from parties with nothing new to say who tonight have formed a lazy alliance in the hope that it passes for coherent opposition.

The leadership of Fine Gael is lazy,

but at least they have a leader. That is more than can be said for the Labour Party. It is utterly leaderless. Nobody knows what their leader stands for but everybody knows what he is against.

MR. [EMMET] STAGG: Is the Minister going to speak about public enterprise at all?

MRS. O'ROURKE: They are against everything. It is a party which has confused initiative with indignation and gets indignant about everything. I have news for Deputy Quinn—there is more to politics than turning red and making one's eyes bulge.

MR. STAGG: The Minister should get back into her bath and cool off.

MRS. O'ROURKE: Occasionally he might consider lowering the mask of mock indignation, dropping the facade of fury and getting real. Deputy Quinn persistently seeks to act out his political life as a misplaced character from 'Noddy gets Narky' and I, for one, have had enough.

AN CEANN COMHAIRLE [SÉAMUS PATTISON]: Deputy Stagg wishes to raise a point of order, what is it?

MR. STAGG: Is it proper for the Minister to deal with everything except the motion—

AN CEANN COMHAIRLE: That is not a point of order. The Deputy will resume his seat.

MRS. O'ROURKE: I have had enough of Deputy Quinn's indignant quivering, enough of his false fury, enough of his bulging bluster. It is time for him to either stand for something or stand aside. The Labour Members can give it but they cannot take it.

To finalise this ragbag of Opposition, this tripartite of trite, we have their strange bedfellows—the Green Party. This party's most momentous decision in its existence has been to finally conclude that it might be a good idea to have a leader. But Deputy Sargent will soon realise that there is more to being a leader than simply putting the name plate on the door, much more to being an environmentalist than retaining a worried frown—

MR. [TREVOR] SARGENT: That is a very personal remark.

MRS. O'ROURKE: There is much more to being a political party than protesting about everything—as we saw last Sunday in Merrion Square—and offering nothing constructive in return.

MR. SARGENT: The Minister was not listening then.

MRS. O'ROURKE: It would be laughable if it were not so serious. This modesty of mediocrity, which has neither policies nor plans is grandly termed the Opposition. The dunce's cap fits. We know what they are opposed to but of what are they in favour? What is their vision of the future? More importantly, how would they achieve their goals if they could focus for even a minute on the goalposts? Does anyone really believe that an Opposition consisting of the three amigos could provide even one coherent policy?

MR. STAGG: I think Deputy O'Dea has written this speech.

MRS. O'ROURKE: What this trio are about today is the politics of the breakfast cereal. The solutions are easy and fast—just add milk. How else could Snap, Crackle and Pop have managed to become leaders of their own parties?

I stand here on my record as Minister for Public Enterprise. The Department teams and my colleagues have worked tirelessly in delivering sustainable public enterprise.

MR. [BRENDAN] HOWLIN:

Will there be any mention of Aer Lingus?

MR. SARGENT:

Or the buses.

MRS. O'ROURKE:

What is Deputy Howlin's plan? Does he intend to hit the Commission in the face? I have attached the real record of progress across the divisions in my Department. If there is one thing I hate it is cowardice. Deputies Noonan and Quinn hightailed it out of Dáil Éireann tonight because they could not bear to hear the truth about themselves. I now formally challenge the three Opposition Leaders, or their party spokespersons, to debate my record in office in any forum.

'THE ENTHUSIASTIC AND WILLING HANDMAIDEN'

'The most scurrilous allegations I have ever heard'

There was uproar in the Dáil in November 2001 when a TD who had rarely spoken in the chamber claimed former Fine Gael Justice Minister Nora Owen should be investigated. Independent Tom Gildea, from Donegal South West, produced no evidence to support his allegation that she was an 'enthusiastic and willing handmaiden' of a cable company. Mrs. Owen rushed from her office to insist he withdraw 'those disgraceful charges' as there was no truth to the allegations whatsoever.

The Dáil was debating an Opposition proposal that a tribunal be established into allegations of garda misconduct in Donegal (the Morris Tribunal would open the following year). Mr. Gildea briefly spoke about members of the McBrearty family, who complained about Garda harrassment after being arrested following the death of cattle dealer Richie Barron. Then he referred to the Diver family in his constituency. They alleged wrongful arrest after a portacabin with £80,000 worth of equipment belonging to Cable Management Ireland was found burnt down. The company had the franchise to rebroadcast

British television stations, which community groups had been transmitting for years using a low-cost deflector system.

Mr. Gildea initially refused to withdraw his charges against Mrs. Owen but subsequently did so. He then voted with the Government against the motion. The Government side won by just one vote.

(21 November 2001)

MR. [TOM] GILDEA: I would like to expand on the role of the Minister for Justice in the rainbow coalition on all these matters pertaining to Garda activities in south west Donegal from 13 December 1995 up to its dissolution in 1997. It was during Deputy Owen's term of office that a force of up to 100 gardaí was amassed for use against the local law abiding rural population of the Ardara-Glenties area. At a later date, almost one year later, the burning of the portacabin and the finding of an explosive device at the site of the proposed MMDS transmission site led to the controversial arrest, detention and interrogation of the Diver family.

On that point, the role of the then Minister for Justice, Deputy Owen, in these matters should be examined. The Garda Síochána in County Donegal was subjected to unacceptable pressure by her.

MR. [PAT] RABBITTE: On a point of order—

MR. GILDEA: She was not only using her powers—

ACTING CHAIRMAN [LIZ McMANUS]: I am sorry, Deputy, but there is a point of order.

MR. RABBITTE: I hate to interrupt a maiden speech, but is the Deputy supporting the request for the tribunal of inquiry or trying to have a tribunal of inquiry into the previous Minister—

ACTING CHAIRMAN: I am sorry, but that is not a point of order.

MR. [MICHAEL] O'KENNEDY: That seems like a maiden speech from Deputy Rabbitte—

ACTING CHAIRMAN: Please allow Deputy Gildea to continue.

MR. O'KENNEDY: —if he thinks that is a point of order. That is a disgrace.

ACTING CHAIRMAN: Deputy O'Kennedy should allow Deputy Gildea to continue.

MR. O'KENNEDY: Deputy Rabbitte is very innocent.

MR. GILDEA:

Deputy Owen was not only using her powers as Minister for Justice to use the Garda, but in actual fact abusing them in dealing with the Garda in County Donegal. I request that she be fully investigated, because as the enthusiastic and willing handmaiden of Cable Management Ireland—

MR. [JIM] HIGGINS:

Who wrote that for the Deputy?

MR. GILDEA:

—she had received financial remuneration. Therefore, it is not only the Garda which should be investigated, but also its political masters during 1996 and 1997. I am seeking a criminal investigation that will result in prosecution—

(Interruptions.)

ACTING CHAIRMAN:

Please allow the Deputy to speak.

(Interruptions.)

MR. O'KENNEDY:

Deputy Rabbitte is preventing the Deputy from making a maiden speech to make his case.

MR. RABBITTE:

Those charges are—

(Interruptions.)

ACTING CHAIRMAN: The Deputy should, please, resume his seat.

MR. RABBITTE: On a point of order, the charges made by the Deputy may only be made by way of substantive motion.

MR. GILDEA: I am seeking a criminal investigation that will result in prosecution rather than a public inquiry. I ask a question of the House. If all Members genuinely want the perpetrators of the injustices—

(Interruptions.)

MR. GILDEA: —inflicted on people in County Donegal to be brought before the courts, regardless of whether the perpetrators are Members of the House—

ACTING CHAIRMAN: May I interrupt the Deputy? It is important that he does not make charges against other Members of the House. He is in need of that advice at this stage.

MR. RABBITTE: He has already made them.

MRS. [NORA] OWEN: I ask Deputy Gildea to give way. I was in my room having come from a meeting and heard him make a disgraceful allegation against me. I want to have it withdrawn now or I will have the House brought to a close after the Ceann Comhairle comes in.

ACTING CHAIRMAN: Will Deputy Gildea withdraw the allegation?

MRS. OWEN: At no stage did I, as Minister for Justice, order, coerce or demand that gardaí, either singly or in multiples, go anywhere. I did not order the Garda to do anything. I would like Deputy Gildea to withdraw that statement. It is a lie for which he has no evidence.

ACTING CHAIRMAN: Is Deputy Gildea willing to withdraw the statement he made?

MR. GILDEA: No.

MRS. OWEN: I will not allow my good name to be besmirched in this way by Deputy Gildea. I am surprised by this. He cannot produce any evidence. There is no evidence that I ordered or mobilised gardaí to go anywhere.

ACTING CHAIRMAN: I ask the Deputy to resume her seat. May I explain to Deputy Gildea—

MR. RABBITTE: On a point of order, with due respect

to the Chair, it is time the Ceann Comhairle was brought into the House. I am absolutely appalled that the Minister for Justice, Equality and Law Reform sat on his hands while these charges were being made and that a Deputy of the longevity of Deputy O'Kennedy has come in to try to support the most outrageous allegations that I have ever heard made and not by way of substantive motion.

ACTING CHAIRMAN: I will suspend the sitting for ten minutes.

[Sitting suspended at 7.40 p.m. and resumed at 7.50 p.m.]

MR. [ALAN] SHATTER: In the course of his contribution this evening Deputy Gildea made outrageous and scandalous charges against Deputy Owen of illegal and corrupt practices which are totally untrue and completely outside any terms in which a Member of this House should speak. We request that Deputy Gildea be required to withdraw the charges he made which are simply designed to cover up his failure to seek to support the motion to enable a tribunal of inquiry to take place. His comments are unacceptable and contrary to the rules of this House.

AN CEANN COMHAIRLE [SÉAMUS PATTISON]: The House had to be suspended due to disorder.

MR. [BRENDAN] HOWLIN: No, it did not.

MR. SHATTER: No, we asked for you, Sir, in the context of comments made by Deputy Gildea.

MR. HOWLIN: Accusations of criminality.

AN CEANN COMHAIRLE: I cannot rule on something I did not hear.

(Interruptions.)

AN CEANN COMHAIRLE: I cannot. This is ridiculous.

(Interruptions.)

MR. SHATTER: A charge has been levelled against a Member of my party, the nature of which, were it any other Member of the House, you would require that it be withdrawn or the Member leave the House. We insist that we have the same protection of the Chair as other Members in circumstances in which a

Deputy wilfully abuses his privileges as a Member of this House.

AN CEANN COMHAIRLE:

When the allegations were made, that was the time to call for the charge to be withdrawn.

MR. SHATTER:

It was. It was raised immediately on a point of order and you were sent for.

(Interruptions.)

MR. SHATTER:

The Acting Chairman requested that Deputy Gildea withdraw his remarks and he failed to do so.

MS. MCMANUS:

I was in the Chair when this happened. It was clear that serious allegations had been made by Deputy Gildea. Deputy Owen entered the House and asked that the allegations be withdrawn. I offered Deputy Gildea the opportunity and asked and advised him to withdraw the allegations, but he did not do so. I am very limited in what I can do in the Chair, which is the reason you were called.

MR. RABBITTE:

I suggest the House be adjourned again until you are given the transcript.

AN CEANN COMHAIRLE:

I cannot pass judgment on this. There is a way to deal with the matter.

(Interruptions.)

MR. RABBITTE: I was in the House at the time. I rose in an attempt to prevent Deputy Gildea proceeding with the most scurrilous allegations I have ever heard during my time in this House. Normally, I would have expected the Minister for Justice, Equality and Law Reform to intervene. He did not. Deputy O'Kennedy made an ass of himself by seeming to support Deputy Gildea. This is so serious, a Cheann Comhairle, that if you have not seen the tape or read the transcript, the House will need to be adjourned until such time as you consider yourself to be in a position to adjudicate on the charges made by Deputy Gildea.

'SLITHERING POLITICAL LIZARD'

As Rabbitte said to Roche

A tetchy day's business focusing on the issue of abortion culminated in a bitter row in February 2002. Michael Noonan, the then leader of Fine Gael, asked Taoiseach Bertie Ahern if he stood over the 'outrageous remarks' a minister had made on radio. Mr. Noonan claimed that the then Marine Minister Frank Fahey had said the abortion referendum was proposed because the Government wanted to stop 'significant numbers' of women seeking to terminate pregnancies on the grounds of suicide. Mr. Fahey denied saying the Government had information that this was happening. The Taoiseach then clashed with Liz McManus and her Labour colleagues, saying, 'I happen to think that pro-life means something . . . You are not a pro-life party; you are a pro-abortion party; you are a pro-choice party'.

Fine Gael TD Nora Owen then insisted Dick Roche of Fianna Fáil withdraw a 'slur' she accused him of levelling against Ms. McManus. Mr. Roche afterwards denied having accused her of being 'pro-abortionist'. The Ceann Comhairle said he could not rule on the alleged comment because he had not heard it. When Mrs. Owen persisted, she was ordered to leave the House. The Ceann Comhairle later suspended the sitting and listened to a recording of the row but could hear no trace of the alleged offensive remark. When Mr. Roche rose to make a statement on what he had actually said, Labour's Pat Rabbitte called him a 'slithering political lizard'.

(13 February 2002)

MR. [PAT] RABBITTE: This is a fine state of affairs.

MRS. [NORA] OWEN: The Ceann Comhairle allowed a thug to insult a decent Member.

AN CEANN COMHAIRLE [SÉAMUS PATTISON]: I ask the Deputy to leave for continually disobeying the Chair. She has refused to accept the Chair's ruling.

MRS. OWEN: I wished to raise a point of order about the Deputy's behaviour. I should not be put out and the Deputy opposite should stop sneering. He is a thug.

MR. RABBITTE: The Ceann Comhairle cannot hear what is being said on those benches but he can hear Deputy Owen. It is a disgrace.

AN CEANN COMHAIRLE: The Deputy should leave the House.

MRS. OWEN: A thug was allowed to insult another Member of this House. It is a disgrace.

MR. [MICHAEL] RING: The Deputy should be ashamed of himself.

MRS. OWEN: He should be ashamed of himself and his leader should be ashamed of himself.

AN CEANN COMHAIRLE: The Deputy must leave.

MR. [JIM] O'KEEFFE: Why was the other Deputy not asked to leave? It is disgraceful.

AN CEANN COMHAIRLE: The Chair has explained the position.

[Mrs. Owen withdrew from the Chamber.]

MR. RABBITTE: This is a disgrace. Deputy Owen was defending the good name of Deputy McManus.

MR. RING: The Deputy opposite should be ashamed of himself.

AN CEANN COMHAIRLE: The Deputy must resume his seat or I will ask him to leave the House.

(Interruptions.)

Mr. [Dick] Roche: That is something coming from a thug and a gurrier.

Mr. Stagg: Did the Ceann Comhairle hear that remark?

Mr. Roche: I withdraw the remark.

Mr. Ring: He does not know how to apologise.

Mr. Roche: I said, 'a thug and a gurrier'.

Mr. Stagg: Has the Ceann Comhairle gone deaf? Did he not hear that remark?

(Interruptions.)

Ms. McManus: The Deputy withdrew that remark but not the one concerning me.

An Ceann Comhairle: I am trying to listen to everyone. Will Deputy Roche resume his seat? Deputy Noonan to speak.

Ms. McManus: Did the Ceann Comhairle not hear what was said? He will not withdraw the slur on my character.

Mr. J. O'Keeffe: The Ceann Comhairle should check the record.

AN CEANN COMHAIRLE:	I called Deputy Noonan and my attention was on him. I did not hear any remark because I was concentrating on Deputy Noonan.
MS. MCMANUS:	A Cheann Comhairle—
AN CEANN COMHAIRLE:	The Deputy must resume her seat.
MR. [MICHAEL] NOONAN:	We have come to a position where Deputies who give offence remain in the House and are protected by the Chair and Deputies who are offended—
AN CEANN COMHAIRLE:	That is not true.
MR. [ALAN] SHATTER:	It is true.
AN CEANN COMHAIRLE:	The Deputy should not accuse the Chair. It is a long-standing rule of the House that unless the Chair hears the offending remark it cannot be ruled on.
MR. NOONAN:	I ask the Ceann Comhairle to adjourn the House to give himself the opportunity to listen to the official recording.

AN CEANN COMHAIRLE:	We will proceed with the business of the House.
MR. NOONAN:	Deputy Owen was put out of the House for—
AN CEANN COMHAIRLE:	For gross disorder.
MR. NOONAN:	—defending the reputation of Deputy McManus from the Deputy from Wicklow who has a constituency interest in smearing her.
DEPUTIES:	Hear, hear.
MR. NOONAN:	That is the situation.
AN CEANN COMHAIRLE:	The Deputy must resume his seat as he has made his point.
MR. HOWLIN:	The Ceann Comhairle has no control of the House.
AN CEANN COMHAIRLE:	The Deputy is making a charge against the Chair which should be withdrawn. It is unworthy of him.
MR. NOONAN:	I am not laying a charge against the Chair, but am stating the fact that Deputy Roche made a scandalous allegation against Deputy McManus.

MR. HOWLIN:	He should admit that.
MR. NOONAN:	Deputy Owen defended Deputy McManus's reputation and was thrown out of the House for her trouble. Meanwhile the main offender sits on the bench opposite smirking.
MR. RING:	Yes, smiling.
MR. NOONAN:	He then laid charges against Deputy Ring and others. I ask the Ceann Comhairle to adjourn the House because this is an injustice—
AN CEANN COMHAIRLE:	I have explained. The Chair is not going to adjourn the House as there is business to be proceeded with.
MR. RING:	The Deputy opposite is allowed to carry on in a disorderly way.
AN CEANN COMHAIRLE:	It is a long-standing rule that if the Chair did not hear the remark, then he cannot rule on it.
MR. [EMMET] STAGG:	The Ceann Comhairle can use modern technology to assist him.
MR. SHATTER:	The Ceann Comhairle should adjourn the House. He was willing to listen to the tape in the matter of Deputy Gildea.

AN CEANN COMHAIRLE:	The Deputy should resume his seat and allow business to continue.
MR. NOONAN:	On a point of order—
AN CEANN COMHAIRLE:	The Deputy must resume his seat. The Deputy cannot have a point of order while the Chair is on his feet. The Deputy may speak briefly.
MR. NOONAN:	Is it not a fundamental principle of the role of Ceann Comhairle that he first and foremost protects Members' interests?
AN CEANN COMHAIRLE:	The Chair will not listen to a lecture from the Deputy.
MR. NOONAN:	I asked a question.
AN CEANN COMHAIRLE:	Will the Deputy resume his seat?
MR. NOONAN:	How can the Ceann Comhairle preside over a situation where a decent Deputy is thrown out of the House while another Deputy who insults a Member is allowed to stay?
AN CEANN COMHAIRLE:	The Deputy must not criticise the Chair, which acted in accordance with long-standing practice in this matter.

MR. NOONAN:

There are precedents, a Cheann Comhairle.

(Interruptions.)

AN CEANN COMHAIRLE:

The Chair will not enter into any further discussion.

[Sitting suspended at 11.15 a.m. and resumed at 11.30 a.m.]

AN CEANN COMHAIRLE:

I took the opportunity to have the tapes carefully listened to and understand there is no trace of the alleged offending remark which cannot be heard. In the circumstances, I intend to proceed with the business of the House.

MR. ROCHE:

A Cheann Comhairle—

AN CEANN COMHAIRLE:

The Chair is addressing the House. It will be necessary for me as Ceann Comhairle to return to this matter and to clarify the position which might arise in similar circumstances. I will return to the matter as quickly as possible. I propose to proceed with the business of the House.

MR. [RÚAIRÍ] QUINN:

On a point of order, I invite Deputy Roche to make a statement. The

House clearly heard his offensive remarks. If the electronic and audio equipment did not pick it up because of interruptions, it still stands in the House as far as we are concerned. I ask Deputy Roche to make a formal statement.

MR. ROCHE: That is what I am trying to do. During the debate I made it clear that my interpretation of the policy of the Labour Party is that it is now pro-choice.

MR. QUINN: Can we have a withdrawal?

MR. ROCHE: The leader of the Labour Party asked me to make a statement, but he is now doing what he always does.

AN CEANN COMHAIRLE: The Deputy should make a brief statement.

MR. ROCHE: My understanding of the Labour Party view is that it is pro-choice, therefore, it is pro-abortion.

MR. RABBITTE: That is not what the Deputy said.

MR. ROCHE: My precise words were that if the Labour Party is for abortion, it should have the honesty to say it is for abortion.

MR. RABBITTE: That is a total distortion.

MR. HOWLIN: That compounds it.

MR. ROCHE: I wrote the words down. I am fairly precise in my choice of language. Deputy Owen then called me a thug.

MR. RABBITTE: The Deputy is a slithering political lizard.

HORLICKS AND RYVITA ALL ROUND!

John Deasy goes up against Michael McDowell — with disastrous results

In February 2003, Fine Gael's then Justice Spokesman John Deasy took a verbal battering from the Minister for Justice, Michael McDowell. Deputy Deasy had attempted to criticise the Minister during a debate on crime levels. But Mr. McDowell claimed he faced a string of 'banal and foolish suggestions' from Fine Gael deputies who 'stuttered and stumbled their way through a series of childish criticisms'. He hit out at the 'sad' idea that alcohol be banned from State functions saying, 'Puerile, ill thought out proposals of that kind do Fine Gael no credit as a political party—Horlicks and Ryvita for everybody.'

Like an irate cat toying with a ball of wool, Mr. McDowell concluded with this withering put down.

'It is a sad spectacle of a bankrupt political party which has decided, in a moment of foolishness, to take me on in regard to this issue. If Deputy Deasy proposes to beat the drum and to take me on he will have to do an awful lot better than he did this evening.'

(25 February 2003)

MR. [MICHAEL] McDowell:	When I came to address this motion I thought I was facing a serious effort by Fine Gael to express its views on the issue of criminal law. Instead, I have had a scatter gun approach of eight Deputies taking five minute soundbites to echo empty comments on the criminal law system.
MR. [PAUL] CONNAUGHTON:	That is a good start Minister.
MR. [BERNARD] DURKAN:	The Minister is a master of soundbites himself.
MR. McDowell:	I found it remarkable that I should come into the House and face such a phalanx of half thought out, negative and insubstantial criticism. It is sad that this is what I face this evening.
MR. [JOHN] PERRY:	The Minister should then explain the Bill to us.
MR. McDowell:	If this is the best the Opposition can do on a serious issue I am sorry for the people who voted for it.
MR. [JOHN] DEASY:	Is that the best the Minister can do for street violence?
MR. McDowell:	Deputy Deasy has been congratulated

by some of the eight people who followed him on his choice of subject. I agree. I think his choice of subject is correct. Unfortunately, none of them put ten minutes work into his or her speech or came up with anything of substance in this debate. It is a disgrace and—

MR. DURKAN: The Minister has been in power for seven months and has done nothing.

ACTING CHAIRMAN [DAVID STANTON]: The Minister without interruption.

MR. MCDOWELL: It is a sad spectacle when Opposition Members will not put five or ten minutes work into preparing a decent speech.

MR. DURKAN: The Minister should look at the reflection in the mirror and get on with the job.

ACTING CHAIRMAN: The Minister without interruption, please.

MR. MCDOWELL: I have not heard one novel idea or original thought but I have heard a lot of gas, noise and shouting. The Opposition is ashamed that I am pointing out the truth this evening. It is a sad let down for the people that the largest Opposition party comes into the House unprepared and without ideas. It is sad that the Opposition comes in unprepared and that one Deputy after another stands and berates me in a puerile and ill thought out way.

MR. DEASY: How much thought did the Minister put into the Bill?

(Interruptions.)

ACTING CHAIRMAN: Order, please.

MR. MCDOWELL: Deputy Deasy really gets the brass neck award. He stood up the other day and said he would prevent citizens of this State who reach the age of 18 from going for a drink. He wanted to make it illegal for them to drink until they were 20. It beggars belief that he should tell me I am out of touch with reality. He should cop himself on. People who have the right to vote have the right to go for a drink.

MR. DURKAN: He is right. The Minister is out of touch.

MR. DEASY: Should we let the county councils extend opening hours until 2 a.m.?

ACTING CHAIRMAN:	Order, please.
MR. McDOWELL:	We will come to that in a moment. I am dealing with what the Deputy proposed. Most people laughed up their sleeves when they heard that suggestion. If that is the best the Deputy can do it is a sad reflection on him.
MR. DURKAN:	What about a Minister sitting seven months and doing nothing?
ACTING CHAIRMAN:	Order, please.
MR. McDOWELL:	Then we had an equally sad suggestion that alcohol should be dropped at Government and State dinners. Fine Gael may be fit for the Horlicks stakes but we intend to live an ordinary civilised way in society. Puerile, ill thought out proposals of that kind do Fine Gael no credit as a political party—Horlicks and Ryvita for everybody.
MR. CONNAUGHTON:	Let us hear the Minister's views. Let him get down to business.
MR. McDOWELL:	I would appreciate it if the Deputies opposite ever read or listened to anything I said. What I said is that if we fix some maximum hour for the

country by which all public houses have to close we should also allow communities, through their local representatives, to choose whether they want an earlier hour than that. I have been attacked for being out of touch in regard to these matters—

MR. DEASY: That is not what the Minister's Department is saying.

MR. McDOWELL: Yes it is. Deputy Deasy is again displaying his lack of knowledge of the situation. Under the Gaming and Lotteries Act, for instance, local authorities are given the right to decide whether or not they will permit gaming arcades in their area. This is something we can do in the Department if we wish. The total vacuity and lack of thought that characterises the Opposition's approach to this debate is represented by this suggestion.

MR. DURKAN: Will the Minister inform us of his approach?

MR. McDOWELL: The obvious logic of what the Opposition is saying is that there must be one hour set for the whole State and there can be no departure from it, that what goes in Temple Bar must go in Templemore. That is the Opposition's approach to the issues that arise in regard to drinking hours. I remind the Deputies that when most of them were here two years ago they strongly supported the opening hours they now claim are a mistake.

MR. CONNAUGHTON: That is a fact.

MR. McDOWELL: Deputy Connaughton, at least, has the honesty to admit it. Fine Gael did not have any doubts on the issue then.

MR. DURKAN: Let the Minister tell us what he proposes.

MR. McDOWELL: Deputy Durkan will have time later to contribute to this debate.

ACTING CHAIRMAN: Order, please. The Minister without interruption.

MR. McDOWELL: If the Deputies honestly believe that there should be one closing hour for the whole State I accept that point of view. However, if they do not believe that, they should have the moral courage to consider it possible that local authorities should be given some discretion as to whether they want their town to be a late night town or not. That is a reasonable proposal. At the moment we give the Judiciary, without local democratic input, the right to give special extensions to night clubs. The local communities' views are immaterial in that process. If one applies to the local district judge one can run a night club that will stay open until 2 a.m. Surely we are at the stage where local public representatives should have some input into that decision in their own community.

I was particularly struck by what one Deputy said. He said that if I knew anything about the way in which decisions are made in local authorities I would not make such a suggestion. I have faith in local representatives and I believe they should represent their communities and make important decisions for them.

MR. DEASY: The Minister is passing the buck.

MR. MCDOWELL: I want to get to the meat of this debate even though the Opposition has not produced much meat for me to deal with. The essence of local democracy is that public representatives can make decisions which have an effect on their local community.

MR. DEASY: The Minister should reform the

managers Act.

MR. McDOWELL: It is a sad state of affairs that Deputy Deasy can do no better than to come up with the puerile, facile suggestion that citizens aged 18 and 19 should not be allowed have a pint in a pub.

Rapid Withdrawal

The Labour leader 'loses it'

Labour leader Pat Rabbitte's long-standing frustration with what he perceived as Ceann Comhairle Dr. Rory O'Hanlon's over rigid adherence to Dáil procedures boiled over into anger on 2 June 2004. The Taoiseach was away on EU business that day and Joe Walsh, the then Minister for Agriculture, was deputising for him in the Dáil. With the local and European elections just days away, he claimed voters he'd met on the hustings were 'in a very buoyant mood'. 'What are they growing?' wondered Michael D. Higgins.

But the tone of the debate changed when Mr. Rabbitte appealed to Dr. O'Hanlon to help him get answers from Mr. Walsh about the closure of rural garda stations, asking how that could be reconiled with the decentralisation programme. Dr. O'Hanlon told Mr. Rabbitte he had broken the rules by asking two questions when he was only entitled to ask one. The Labour leader exploded in fury. He accused Dr. O'Hanlon of being 'partisan' and said he was 'congenitally incapable of being fair'. Communications Minister Dermot Ahern suggested that Mr. Rabbitte was 'losing it'. Before leaving the chamber, the Labour leader said he wouldn't take advice from that 'boot-boy from Dundalk'.

(The next day Dr. O'Hanlon warned deputies, 'I have no intention of allowing the Chair to be intimidated and deflected from doing his duty.')

(02 June 2004)

MR. [PAT] RABBITTE:	. . . I asked one question about Garda stations and I did not get an answer. I merely pointed out the conflict of closing rural Garda stations and post offices with a professed commitment to decentralisation. With all due respect, I will explain what I am asking without help from you.
AN CEANN COMHAIRLE [RORY O'HANLON]:	Sorry, Deputy—
MR. RABBITTE:	You are the most partisan Chair this House has ever had.
AN CEANN COMHAIRLE:	Deputy—
MR. RABBITTE:	I asked questions about Garda stations and I am merely pointing out—

AN CEANN COMHAIRLE:	I ask the Deputy to withdraw the remark that the Chair is partisan.
MR. RABBITTE:	I am merely pointing out to you—
AN CEANN COMHAIRLE:	Deputy, I am asking you to withdraw the remark.
MR. [DERMOT] AHERN:	He is losing it.
MR. RABBITTE:	I am not losing it and I do not want advice from the boot-boy from Dundalk.
AN CEANN COMHAIRLE:	Deputy Rabbitte, I ask you to withdraw the remark that the Chair is partisan.
MR. RABBITTE:	A Cheann Comhairle, time after time you intervene to protect the Government.
AN CEANN COMHAIRLE:	Deputy, I am asking you to withdraw the remark.
MR. RABBITTE:	Time after time, you do it virtually every day and I am sick of it.
AN CEANN COMHAIRLE:	Deputy, I am asking you to withdraw the remark.

MR. RABBITTE:	I am sick of your partisan approach.
AN CEANN COMHAIRLE:	Deputy, I am asking you—
MR. RABBITTE:	You are congenitally incapable of being fair.
AN CEANN COMHAIRLE:	If the Deputy does not withdraw the remarks, he knows the options. I ask you to withdraw the remarks.
MR. RABBITTE:	I asked about Garda stations and I got no answer.
AN CEANN COMHAIRLE:	Deputy, before you proceed, do you intend to withdraw the remarks?
MR. RABBITTE:	I will not withdraw the remarks because you are unfair every day.
AN CEANN COMHAIRLE:	Deputy—
MR. RABBITTE:	You intervene to protect the Government at every opportunity.
AN CEANN COMHAIRLE:	Deputy, I ask you to withdraw that remark.
MR. RABBITTE:	I will not withdraw it. You are disgracefully partisan.

AN CEANN COMHAIRLE:	All right, Deputy.
MR. RABBITTE:	I am sick of it.
AN CEANN COMHAIRLE:	As you are the leader of a party, the Chair intends to give you time.
MR. RABBITTE:	Any time you can intervene to protect the Government, you intervene. The Minister did not answer one iota of the question I asked about Garda stations.
AN CEANN COMHAIRLE:	I intend to give you time, Deputy, to consider your position before you are asked to leave the House.
MR. RABBITTE:	I asked about Garda stations and the Minister did not answer one aspect of the question, then you give me a lecture about decentralisation.
AN CEANN COMHAIRLE:	I am suspending the sitting for five minutes.
MR. RABBITTE:	You can suspend what you like.
	[The Dáil was suspended for five minutes]
AN CEANN COMHAIRLE:	Deputy Rabbitte, once again I request that you withdraw your remark.

MR. RABBITTE:
I am sorry my remarks led to disruption of the House, but I regret I cannot withdraw them. I will withdraw from the House rather than do so.

[Mr. Rabbitte left the Chamber.]

'Tiny Little Bigot'

Ó Snodaigh vs Cullen — as Gaeilge

artin Cullen, who was Environment Minister at the time of this spat, challenged Sinn Féin's Aengus Ó Snodaigh to repeat allegations of corruption against him outside the privilege of the Dáil in June 2004. (TDs cannot be sued for defamation over any speech in the House.) Mr. Ó Snodaigh claimed Mr. Cullen was a 'tiny little bigot' bent on destroying Irish heritage. Mr. Cullen rounded on Sinn Féin, saying the party 'knee-caps people who do not agree with it'. The row erupted during a debate on the bill allowing for the completion of the M50 motorway at Carrickmines.

Earlier in the debate Deputy Ó Snodaigh spoke mostly in Irish—despite Mr. Cullen's protests that he didn't have the same facility in the language as his opponent.

(22 June 2004)

MR. [MARTIN] CULLEN:

The Deputy would have worn brown shirts in the thirties. He should grab the banners and have a private army. That is what he wants. He wants a private army to back up everything he does. He will not get away with it. Sinn Féin will not get away with it.

MR. [AENGUS] Ó SNODAIGH:

Ní gá dúinn aon airm a bheith againn in san cheist seo. Tá an cheist seo an simplí. An tAire an duine a scriosfaidh oidhreacht na hÉireann. Cad atá an Rialtas ag trialladh a dhéanamh amuigh i gCluain Dolcáin? Tá siad sásta cead a thabhairt do thógálaí—

MR. CULLEN:

He is in here shouting and roaring while his private army is outside the door to back up everything he says.

AN LEAS-CHEANN COMHAIRLE [SÉAMUS PATTISON]:

Order, please. The Deputy should be allowed make his speech without interruption.

MR. Ó SNODAIGH:

Is é an tAire a thosaigh an screadaíl. Is trua nach n-aithníonn sé oidhreacht a pháirtí féin. Ba chóir dó smaoineamh ar oidhreacht Fhianna Fáil.

MR. CULLEN:

That is old cleverality. He should tell that to what is left of the Marxist Communist group in Europe that his party has joined. Their failed old policies never delivered a job, built a house or did anything for anybody. That is all Sinn Féin is interested in.

AN LEAS-CHEANN COMHAIRLE:

The Minister is being disorderly.

MR. Ó SNODAIGH:

Ní dhearna an tAire mórán ach oiread ach airgead a thabhairt do rachmasaithe agus a bheith ag cruinniú airgid. Sin an méid a dhein an tAire agus sin an méid atá ag teacht ón Rialtas. Sin an fáth nach bhfuil an tAire sásta éisteacht leis an gceist. Tá sé ag iarraidh mise a mhaslú. Is cuma liom.

MR. CULLEN:

The Deputy is not at one of his back-room lectures being told what to do and when to do it.

MR. Ó SNODAIGH:

Is féidir leis mise a mhaslú de shíor. Ní chuireann sin as dom.

MR. CULLEN:

We live in a democracy.

MR. Ó SNODAIGH:

Cuireann sé as dom nach bhfuil an tAire sásta na ceisteanna atá á n-ardú agam a fhreagairt nó fiú éisteacht leo. Sin cé chomh maslach is atá an tAire. Is cuma liom. Tá an tAire ag maslú mhuintir na hÉireann. Cé gur Aire de mhuintir na hÉireann é níl sé sásta éisteacht leis na pointí a ardaítear ar an gceist seo. Sin cé chomh gránna is atá sé. Slibhín beag bídeach is ea é. Ní bheidh a ainm thíos amach anseo. Beidh sé gránna. Smaoineofar air mar loitiméir na tíre, loitiméir na staire agus loitiméir na hoidhreachta. Sin a bhfuil sé tar éis a dhéanamh.

MR. CULLEN: That describes Sinn Féin and their carry-on.

MR. Ó SNODAIGH: I am talking about the Minister.

MR. CULLEN: The Deputy should look in the mirror.

AN LEAS-CHEANN COMHAIRLE: The Minister is being disorderly.

MR. CULLEN: His party knee-caps people who do not agree with it. They terrorise people. They are the experts in building concrete bunkers.

AN LEAS-CHEANN COMHAIRLE: The Minister is being disorderly.

MR. Ó SNODAIGH: If the Minister wants a debate on that subject or any subject he should order time through his Whip.

AN LEAS-CHEANN COMHAIRLE:	Members should address the Chair.
MR. Ó SNODAIGH:	If the Minister wishes to have a debate on any other subject, he is in Government. He can order time for it and I will willingly debate any subject in this House. I am debating this matter and the Minister is insulting me and the Irish people.
MR. CULLEN:	Facts do not get in the way of the Deputy spinning his old yarns.
MR. Ó SNODAIGH:	I have not spun any yarn yet.
MR. CULLEN:	Sinn Féin never does.
MR. Ó SNODAIGH:	The Minister does not even have the intelligence to listen to what I have to say, in Irish or English.
MR. CULLEN:	The Deputy knows I do not have the same facility in Irish that he has.
MR. Ó SNODAIGH:	There he is, shouting again. The Minister has just shown himself to be both simple minded and a bigot who has destroyed our heritage.
MR. CULLEN:	The Deputy should look in the mirror.

MR. Ó SNODAIGH:

I look in the mirror every day and I am proud of what I see. What I see across the Chamber is a tiny little bigot who should be thrown out of the House for continually disrupting me.

MR. CULLEN:

I have plenty of reasons to get at a person, without getting down in the muck.

AN LEAS-CHEANN COMHAIRLE:

Order, please.

MR. Ó SNODAIGH:

The Minister should be ashamed of himself that he will not even answer or listen to the debate on this important matter.

AN LEAS-CHEANN COMHAIRLE:

Will the Minister please stop interrupting?

MR. Ó SNODAIGH:

The Minister is scandalous. He is connected with corruption on his side of the House, as regards people who have taken payments in respect of Jackson Way and other works.

MR. CULLEN:

The Deputy should make that statement outside the House, if he is man enough, or withdraw it.

AN LEAS-CHEANN COMHAIRLE:	The Chair is calling on the Minister to cease interrupting.
MR. Ó SNODAIGH:	I have no problem repeating that outside the House. Who, in the Minister's party, have already been in front of the tribunal?
MR. CULLEN:	Back it up.
MR. Ó SNODAIGH:	I have backed it up. The tribunal is doing its work. These people are connected with the Minister's party, not my party. That is the scandal. That has to do with corruption. Just look at what that is destroying. That is how small-minded the Minister is, and the rest of his party. To destroy the heritage and concrete it over is their solution to everything. The Minister is scandalous and should give up as quickly as possible. He is no Minister for the environment. The only environment he wants is concrete.
AN LEAS-CHEANN COMHAIRLE:	The Deputy should address the Chair.
MR. Ó SNODAIGH:	I will address the Chair if I do not get any more interruptions. If the Minister continues to interrupt I will continue in the same vein. Just in case

the Minister does not understand Irish in any shape or form, I referred to the scandal in Trim, where a multistorey hotel is being built next to a national monument. It is taking away from the national monument. The Minister is supposed to promote national monuments, not allow building on top of or next to them.

MR. CULLEN: The Deputy should state the facts.

MR. Ó SNODAIGH: That is exactly what the Minister is doing.

MR. CULLEN: It is not.

AN LEAS-CHEANN COMHAIRLE: Order, please. The Minister will have the opportunity to reply.

MR. Ó SNODAIGH: A seven storey building is going up across the road from Kilmainham Jail. At the back of it is another ten storey building.

AN LEAS-CHEANN COMHAIRLE: The Deputy will conclude.

MR. Ó SNODAIGH: I conclude by continuing with my claim that the Minister is connected with people in this House who are corrupt, who have forced through Carrickmines.

MR. CULLEN: The Deputy will withdraw that remark or repeat it outside the House.

AN LEAS-CHEANN COMHAIRLE: Order, please.

MR. Ó SNODAIGH: I have repeated it ten times and I will not withdraw it. If the Minister wishes, I will repeat it outside the House.

MR. CULLEN: The Deputy should repeat that outside the House if he is man enough.

AN LEAS-CHEANN COMHAIRLE: Deputies should be allowed to make their contributions without interruption.

MR. [DAMIEN] ENGLISH: That was great. I should have spent more time in Irish class. I could have enjoyed that much more.

PART THREE

War

'THE BASTARDS WHO HAVE BROUGHT IRELAND TO ITS KNEES'

The aftermath of Omagh

The Real IRA detonated a car bomb in Omagh on 15 August 1998. Twenty-nine people and unborn twin girls were killed. The Dáil was recalled to debate emergency legislation, which was easily passed; the amended Offences Against the State Act gave Gardaí new powers to combat paramilitary activity.

During statements on the tragedy, the then Fine Gael leader John Bruton criticised the IRA for not saying 'the war is over' when the words were so 'crucial and very simple'. He asked, 'Why is the Government afraid to ask it to say so? Why is the Government afraid of the answer it will get?'

But the generally restrained tones of the other party leaders' prepared speeches gave way to this fierce contribution from Fine Gael's Brendan McGahon during the debate on the legislation.

And he singled out just three deputies with what he called the 'political balls' to address the problem of violent republicanism.

(02 September 1998)

MR. [BRENDAN] McGAHON:

I do not like to say 'I told you so' but for 16 years I have opposed the IRA in all its forms, in my native town of Dundalk in County Louth in general and in this Chamber. Only two months ago, I was the only Deputy in this House to oppose the release of prisoners. I did so because of my total opposition to terrorism and my belief that it should never be rewarded. Having said that, I wish to express my total support for the measures the Minister is introducing today. However, it is like closing the stable door after the horse has bolted.

The tragedy of Omagh in which so many women and children were killed was such that violent republicanism will be dead in Ireland for several years to come. The rats who have murdered people for the past 30 years have retreated into their bolt holes. Some of them will hopefully be bolted up for good but some will escape. I do not believe violent republicanism is dead. Like Dracula, it would be necessary to drive a stake through its breast to achieve that.

We should seek to inculcate in our people a spirit of nationalism as opposed to republicanism. Republicanism equates with violence. Part of the problem is that generations of

Irish people have been brought up listening to mythical teachings in the schools. We need to foster the kind of nationalism demonstrated by John Redmond, a man who sought a united Ireland through peaceful means.

For 30 years, we have witnessed the appeasement of terror in this country. Politicians are currently jumping on the bandwagon following the horrific slaughter at Omagh. Why were these measures not introduced 30 years ago? Why were they not introduced after Enniskillen in which an equally horrendous assault occurred? Why was action not taken after Warrenpoint in which 18 young men were butchered? The Government was aware of the perpetrators in that instance but the DPP refused to press charges, probably for political reasons. I indict all Governments over the past 30 years, including my own, for being soft on terrorism. They were constantly looking over their shoulders to see if people would approve of the introduction of repressive measures or if such action would be considered politically correct. I am not politically correct and over the past 16 years I have unambiguously opposed the IRA—sometimes under threat to my life and my town.

The former Minister for Justice, Mr. Paddy Cooney, Deputy O'Malley and Deputy John Bruton are the only people in this House with the political balls to address this problem. I hope time will show that the Minister has the same courage. These measures we have been forced to take are an indication of how much out of control this country has been for the past 30 years when death stalked the land—death promoted by Adams and McGuinness, the IRA's chief of staff, who are guilty by association of the deaths of hundreds of Irish people. Now they are being hailed as international statesmen. They are the bastards who have brought Ireland to its knees. They were a cause of this horrendous tragedy and now they pose as international statesmen because they have been sung a song by the British Government, who sing a different song to everybody— including the loyalists—and have done for many years.

Like everyone else I want a peaceful Ireland. I live in the front theatre of it, just two miles from the Border. I have known people from both sides of the Border who have lost their lives, people who have been murdered by various terrorist gangs while we stood idly by. Terrorism has to be confronted and pious platitudes and pleas for people to sit down and rationalise are simply not enough. There must be a deterrent factor. Some time in the future dissent will occur in the Assembly and the IRA terrorists will emerge from their hideaways to kill again. We must accept that society has to be protected by Governments and they should have the courage to govern without looking over their shoulders to see if it is politically expedient to do so.

I wish to dissociate myself from the comments made by Deputy Ó Caoláin when he castigated the Garda Síochána. The organisation to which he belongs has taken the lives of 16 gardaí and seven members of the Irish Army. That is a shameful record. He should hang his head in shame when he makes comments in relation to the fairness of the Garda.

These measures in a normal society would not be necessary but, sadly, we have to recognise that we live in an abnormal society and it is 30 years too late for many people. The Omagh bombing took the lives of 28* people and left many more maimed for life. There have been 3,700 people killed in the North and their lives were as valuable as those of the victims of Omagh. I commend the Minister for belatedly bringing in these measures and I indict my own party for its failure to do so in the years in which it was in power.

[*The final death toll was 29 people. It was 28 people at the time of this speech.]

'LIKE TRYING TO PLAY HANDBALL AGAINST A HAYSTACK'

Higgins struggles for answers from Ahern

In January 2003 Independent Socialist TD Joe Higgins voiced strong opposition to the US military's use of Shannon Airport. He repeatedly quizzed the Taoiseach Bertie Ahern as to whether or not the Government had allowed the Americans to flout regulations governing the transport of weapons. Mr. Ahern said officials did not board aircraft from friendly countries to carry out a precise cargo check.

Paraphrasing a quote heard at the farmers' protest earlier that month, Mr. Higgins claimed that asking Mr. Ahern a question was like trying to play handball against a haystack.

(29 January 2003)

MR. [JOE] HIGGINS: I am reminded of what a farmer said recently about a different member of the Government. Asking the Taoiseach a question is like trying to play handball against a haystack. You hear a dull thud and the ball does not come back to you. It goes all over the world, but it certainly does not come back to the person asking the question.

I would like a specific answer from the Taoiseach. The Taoiseach knows that President Bush, the fundamentalists who surround him and his fellow fundamentalist, Prime Minister Blair, intend to attack Iraq no matter what. He should be very clear that they have made up their minds. He knows that doing so will wreak havoc on the peoples of Iraq and has nothing to do with weapons of mass destruction, but is about oil, power and influence in the world. By colluding with that by facilitating the US military build-up, the Taoiseach will have on his hands the blood of the innocent Iraqi people who will undoubtedly be slaughtered.

The Taoiseach now says that 30 aircraft passing through our airports, mainly Shannon, notified that they were carrying munitions of war and were given permission to land. The other 532 aircraft neither sought nor received permission to carry munitions of war. Will the Taoiseach tell the Dáil that those aeroplanes, whether freight or passenger craft, did not have any weapons on board or munitions designed to wreak havoc on people or property?

THE TAOISEACH [BERTIE AHERN]	I am satisfied the regulations were followed.

MR. J. HIGGINS: What changed last week?

THE TAOISEACH: Due to a recent increase in the number of aircraft, the Minister reiterated the message. What might have changed is that there is a more difficult state of affairs where they are going now. The Deputy says I will not answer his first question. If Saddam Hussein changes the regulations, complies with the inspectors, international law and the UN mandate, we will not have this problem.

MR. J. HIGGINS: It is not about weapons of mass destruction.

THE TAOISEACH: We will not have this problem if he complies in a very friendly way with the inspectors who stated that he has been helpful in process but not in substance. They have urged the Security Council, the USA and the UK to hold back. If he complies with them fully, none of us will have a problem—

Mr. J. Higgins:	The Taoiseach knows what this is about.
The Taoiseach:	—and the Deputy will not have to get excited about it. The Deputy is totally against the United States of America in every regard.
Mr. J. Higgins:	I am not against the United States.
Mr. [Paul] Gogarty:	We are against the Bush Administration.
The Taoiseach:	I am against Saddam Hussein and both of us will get our way.
Mr. J. Higgins:	I have been against Saddam Hussein since before the Taoiseach even knew he existed.
Mr. Gogarty:	The majority of Americans are against this war.
The Taoiseach:	We will not have a war and we will have no difficulties if Saddam Hussein complies with UN Resolution 1441 of 8 November which was passed by all 14 members of the Security Council. The entire world cannot be wrong. One dictator is wrong and he is a man who has used weapons of mass destruction against his own people and who has lost 6,500 chemical

bombs. Let us be realistic. The Deputy should not stand up in this House to defend the indefensible.

MR. J. HIGGINS: Who is defending the indefensible?

MR. [MICHAEL] SMITH: The Deputy is.

THE TAOISEACH: The Deputy should use his energy in the same way as everybody else in the world to see that the UN resolution is complied with. That is what we should be trying to do.

MR. GOGARTY: The Taoiseach is worse than the Vichy Government.

MR. M. SMITH: The Deputy should tell that to the Iranian war veterans.

Michael D.'s War

The Labour Party's WMD takes aim at the government benches

In March 2003, with the Dáil about to adjourn for over three weeks on the eve of war in Iraq, Labour's Foreign Affairs Spokesman Michael D. Higgins silenced the House with this passionate contribution. He denounced the Taoiseach Bertie Ahern for 'fudging' by not expressing an opinion on the impending conflict. And he claimed the Dáil would be 'shamed' for failing to debate the crisis.

Mr. Higgins pointed to the Government benches when he warned that the 'blood of Iraqi children and civilians will be on the hands of all the people who would not permit a discussion on the issue.' His speech was followed by applause from Opposition TDs—and silence from Fianna Fáil and PD deputies.

(12 March 2003)

AN LEAS-CHEANN COMHAIRLE [SÉAMUS PATTISON]	Is the proposal for dealing with the adjournment of the Dáil today agreed?

MR. [MICHAEL D.] HIGGINS:

We have, for two days now, heard a new spin on a commitment given last week that we would have a debate on Iraq. We were told such a debate could take place if there was a change in position. Apart from the fact that that change has taken place, who is to say whether the debate is justified?

I put it to the Taoiseach that there are matters on Iraq that have never been discussed in this House. Neither he nor the Minister for Foreign Affairs, Deputy Cowen, has made one substantial reference in any statement to the Dáil on the humanitarian consequences of a war. Not one paragraph has been devoted to that issue. Yet, by the time this House returns on Tuesday, 25 March it is possible that up to one million mothers may be affected by war, there may be 100,000 direct casualties and 400,000 secondary ones, ten to 15 million people on food dependency may also be affected. That that does not merit a debate in this House is a disgrace.

The Taoiseach is fudging the question on where he stands regarding the illegality or otherwise of a pre-emptive strike and the action by a super State outside the ambit of the United Nations Charter. That matter has not been discussed in this House. The Taoiseach says he is in favour of the United Nations. Is he in favour of the UN Charter? If not, which proposal in the Security Council does he favour? If an illegal action takes place, what is the status of all his previous actions on Shannon?

The Taoiseach as good as said this morning that irrespective of legality or otherwise he will allow Shannon to be used for business purposes. That is a change.

AN LEAS-CHEANN COMHAIRLE:

I take it the Deputy is opposing the proposal.

MR. M. HIGGINS:

I have been a Member of this House for a long time. I do not want it to happen in my name that we went into a long break on the verge of a war that will affect so many people as I have described and will change international politics. The Chief Whip has come up with a cheap suggestion that if matters change we will have a debate. There is time for a debate tonight, tomorrow or next week. I do not want it to happen in my name that this House adjourned on the brink of war, on the verge of illegality with all its consequences not only of a humanitarian kind but of an international legal and political kind. The Government will come back on the 25 March happy in the knowledge that it got away without offering an opinion. One wishes we were members of the Security Council. We might at least have had to make up our mind.

AN LEAS-CHEANN COMHAIRLE:

The Deputy is making a long statement.

MR. M. HIGGINS:

I oppose the Order of Business and will continue to do so.

AN LEAS-CHEANN COMHAIRLE:

A brief statement from the Deputy, please.

MR. M. HIGGINS:

The blood of Iraqi children and civilians will be on the hands of all the people who would not permit a discussion on the issue.

They are the ones who would not allow it to be discussed. This Parliament will have been shamed. It is a disgrace the Taoiseach does not have an opinion and is not having a debate. He is slinking off to the United States half hoping he will give an excuse and will come back with more. It is very wrong.

THE COALITION OF THE WILLING

The Taoiseach 'presumes' Ireland is on Bush's list

The US State Department published a list of 'the coalition of the willing' in March 2003. It contained 30 countries who were prepared to be publicly on the side of America in the event of war in Iraq. Fifteen other States were apparently happy to provide assistance but did not wish to be named.

When war broke out, Labour leader Pat Rabbitte pressed the Taoiseach, Bertie Ahern to 'clarify whether Ireland is included in that *in pectore* list of 15'. Mr. Ahern said he'd had no contact with the US administration since the conflict began. But he'd heard an American official say countries allowing over-flight rights to the US military were included, 'so I presume we would be'. 'So we are members of the coalition of the willing?' asked Mr. Rabbitte. Mr. Ahern said he'd had no contact with the American administration since the conflict began and continued to insist the Government was not supporting any State in the crisis.

(25 March 2003)

THE TAOISEACH:	As regards the Deputy's question concerning the list, I do not know who is on it.
MR. [PAT] RABBITTE:	Are we on it?
THE TAOISEACH:	On Saturday, I heard an American official state that people who allowed overflights would be included so I presume we would be.
MR. RABBITTE:	Are we on the list of 15?
THE TAOISEACH:	I presume then that we would be.
MR. RABBITTE:	We are?
AN CEANN COMHAIRLE [RORY O'HANLON]:	Allow the Taoiseach time to answer the question.
THE TAOISEACH:	I have answered it. I presume we would be.
MR. RABBITTE:	I thought we were not participating.
AN CEANN COMHAIRLE:	I am sorry, Deputy Rabbitte. No more supplementary questions
THE TAOISEACH:	We are not participating in the war, but they include on the list people who are allowing overflight facilities.

MR. RABBITTE:	So we are members of the coalition of the willing?
AN CEANN COMHAIRLE:	Deputy Rabbitte should allow the Taoiseach to conclude.
THE TAOISEACH:	We are not members of the coalition.
MR. RABBITTE:	This is very important because the Irish people did not know that we were part of the coalition of the willing.
THE TAOISEACH:	A Cheann Comhairle, if I could answer Deputy Rabbitte's question.
AN CEANN COMHAIRLE:	Deputy Rabbitte, the Standing Order on Leaders' Questions is quite specific.
MR. RABBITTE:	The Irish people did not know this.
AN CEANN COMHAIRLE:	Deputy Rabbitte, you are out of order. I would ask you to allow the Taoiseach to conclude.
MR. RABBITTE:	I might be out of order but not as out of order as the Government.
AN CEANN COMHAIRLE:	I would ask the Deputy to resume his seat, please.
THE TAOISEACH:	We are not part of the coalition of the

willing.

MR. [TREVOR]
SARGENT:

The Taoiseach is the only one who says that.

THE TAOISEACH:

No, I am not. Our position is accepted in international and domestic law, as well as by the United Nations and the European Union. In fact, very few people have any difficulty in understanding our position, other than Deputy Sargent.

MR. [DAN] BOYLE:

Mr. Rumsfeld has.

THE TAOISEACH:

Our position is that we will not participate in this war—we do not support it—but we totally support the humanitarian relief effort. If Members of the House were serious about the matter they should, as Deputy Kenny has done, turn their attention to the relief issue.

MR. SARGENT:

The humanitarian issue is the reason it is important to pose the questions we are raising. Would the Taoiseach care to correct his statement that the Government does not support any state in this conflict? The Tánaiste was quite clear in saying that we were supporting the United States—'our friends', as she put it. That was very clear to everybody.

'GOD HELP US IF THE GREEN PARTY IS EVER IN CHARGE'

O'Dea denies undermining neutrality

In November 2004 Defence Minister Willie O'Dea and the Green's John Gormley had one of their more heated rows over neutrality. A number of deputies had asked the Minister if Ireland would be participating in EU Battle Groups. He said the State was prepared to consult with European partners on rapid response elements. Mr. Gormley's response was that the Government's commitment to neutrality was about as plausible as its commitment to socialism. 'There is no group as autocratic in this country as liberals,' sighed the Coalition Minister. He went on to describe Mr. Gormley's claim that the Government was undermining Irish neutrality as 'spurious', adding 'God help us if the Green Party, with its present autocratic attitude, is ever in charge'.

(17 November 2004)

MR. [JOHN] GORMLEY: It seems clear from the Minister's response that the Government is committed to EU battle groups. He should come out and say it clearly. Does the Minister agree the Government has done more than any other previous Administration to un-do and dismantle Irish neutrality? We see examples of that in Shannon Airport almost every day. The apparent decision to participate in battle groups is another step in that direction, as is the new EU constitution.

What is Ireland's role in the new European arms agency? Will the battle groups be part of the structured co-operation which forms part of the new European constitution? That important question also needs to be answered. Does the Minister accept that a common defence, as defined in the new EU constitution, is on the way? It is no longer merely possible that we will be involved in a common defence, as the EU constitution states explicitly that we will be part of a common defence. Do these developments not demonstrate that the Government's commitment to neutrality is about as plausible as its commitment to socialism?

MR. [WILLIE] O'DEA: I do not really know what Deputy

Gormley is committed to, on any front.

MR. GORMLEY: I am committed to Irish neutrality.

MR. O'DEA: He is obviously committed to not listening.

MR. GORMLEY: I listened to the Minister.

MR. O'DEA: If he listened carefully to my reply, he would have heard me make clear that I will talk to my European counterparts about the matter on Monday. When I have received answers to the various questions I want to ask—

MR. GORMLEY: The Minister is very predictable.

MR. O'DEA: There is no group as autocratic in this country as liberals. They do not want to hear anybody else's point of view.

MR. GORMLEY: I am listening.

MR. O'DEA: I ask the Deputy to keep listening. I will ask the various questions compiled by the Department, the responses to which we are still evaluating. When I have received the answers to the questions, I will discuss the matter at Cabinet level. I will not make the decision on Ireland's participation in the battle groups. I have views on the matter, but the decision will be taken by the Cabinet.

I reject Deputy Gormley's spurious contention that the Government is undermining neutrality. The Government's definition of neutrality, which has been upheld by the courts, involves non-participation in military alliances. That has been the policy of this country for the last 50 years and it continues to be its policy. Ireland is not involved in any military alliance and it will not be involved in such an alliance. It is not involved in any mutual defence pact and it will not be involved in such a pact. Ireland has not taken any action in respect of Iraq or anywhere else that was not taken by successive Irish Governments over the last 50 years. It is clear that is the reality.

I remind Deputy Gormley that those with certain beliefs are entitled to have them. I allow them to voice their opinions and I wish they would let me voice my opinion, rather than trying to shout me down. As far as I am concerned, such people are entitled to their opinions. I do not send people around in the middle of the night to damage such people's property. My property was damaged on a number of occasions by people who, according to the Garda in Limerick, are associated with Deputy Gormley's party.

MR. GORMLEY: Come on.

MR. O'DEA: My property has been damaged simply because I happen to hold a different opinion.

MR. GORMLEY: That is outrageous.

MR. O'DEA: We live in a democracy. God help us if the Green Party, with its present autocratic attitude, is ever in charge.

MR. GORMLEY: It is outrageous.

MR. O'DEA: Deputy Gormley has asked for various—

MR. GORMLEY: It is outrageous.

MR. O'DEA: It is a matter of fact. If Deputy Gormley does not believe me, I will send him the evidence of the Garda in Limerick.

MR. [AENGUS] Ó SNODAIGH: Charge them.

MR. GORMLEY: Do something.

MR. O'DEA

I will. Deputy Gormley and some of his colleagues in the mid-west who shout the loudest have been asking for a debate on neutrality. I have no difficulty with having such a debate at any time, in any place. I suggest the putative coalition partners in the next Government should have a debate among themselves first, so they can come to me with a common voice.

'GET OVER IT'

Sinn Féin deputies rebuked for praising IRA

S inn Féin TD Caoimhghín Ó Caoláin was heckled when he praised the 'leadership of the Irish Republican Army' in the Dáil in December 2004. Deputies of all parties had expressed frustration at the collapse of the latest round of talks on the North. The failure to seal a deal to restore devolution was this time blamed largely on the dispute over whether or not photographs of IRA decommissioning should be taken and published.

Mr. Ó Caoláin commended the IRA leadership which, he said, had 'clearly demonstrated its preparedness to take historic and unprecedented steps'. He was castigated by other TDs who insisted members of the House recognised only one Army. The Tánaiste Mary Harney said she would not applaud anyone who had carried out dreadful atrocities for far too long. When Sinn Féin's Arthur Morgan asked if that sentiment should also apply to Britain, PD Deputy Liz O'Donnell told him to 'get over it'.

(09 December 2004)

MR. [CAOIMHGHÍN] Ó CAOLÁIN:	I wish to record my disappointment and that of my colleagues at the failure so far to achieve the goal of a full implementation of the Good Friday Agreement, a goal to which our party is absolutely committed. I join other voices in the House in commending the efforts of both Governments and of the Taoiseach and British Prime Minister.

I also strongly commend the courageous efforts of the Sinn Féin leadership and negotiating team who have demonstrated an absolute commitment to the address of all the difficulties that have bedevilled this island and the neighbouring island and our relationship for generations. They have shown themselves to be courageous leaders. I wish also to commend the leadership of the Irish Republican Army which has clearly demonstrated its preparedness to take historic and unprecedented steps.

MS. [JOAN] BURTON: There is only one Army in this country. Dáil Éireann recognises only one Army.

MR Ó CAOLÁIN: That must be acknowledged.

MR. [BRIAN] LENIHAN: For shame.

MR. Ó CAOLÁIN:	I am proud to stand in this House and so record.
MR. [DICK] ROCHE:	Shame on Deputy Ó Caoláin.
MS. [LIZ] O'DONNELL:	Members of this House recognise only one Army.
AN CEANN COMHAIRLE [RORY O'HANLON]:	Allow Deputy Ó Caoláin speak without interruption, please.
MR. Ó CAOLÁIN:	It would serve much better the goal to which, I hope, all voices in this House are committed, although at times it is difficult to recognise that commitment, if utterances were measured because this is unfinished business and a work in train that must be pursued to achieve a satisfactory result acceptable to all sides in the conflict. I urge colleague Deputies to be measured.
THE TÁNAISTE [MARY HARNEY]:	It is important that we are all measured. I would not applaud anyone who killed and maimed in the name of Ireland and carried out dreadful atrocities for far too long.
DEPUTIES:	Hear, hear.
THE TÁNAISTE:	The majority of people in this

country and this House only pursued constitutional politics.

MR. [ARTHUR] MORGAN: Does the Tánaiste extend that sentiment to include Britain?

MS. O'DONNELL: Deputy Morgan should get over it.

EVENTS HAVE TAKEN A BAD TURN

The Taoiseach rounds on Sinn Féin

The Taoiseach Bertie Ahern gave this understated assessment of the grave state of the peace process when the Dáil resumed in January 2005, 'Events have taken a bad turn.' He said he accepted intelligence reports that the previous month's £22 million Northern Bank raid was carried out by the Provisional IRA. And he believed an operation of that scale could not have been undertaken without the knowledge of the Provo leadership.

Indicating a change in his attitude towards Sinn Féin, he conceded that 'all kinds of things' had been ignored in the past but now 'things must be equal'. Sinn Féin's Caoimhghín Ó Caoláin claimed Mr. Ahern's 'outbursts and allegations' were motivated by the electoral threat his party was posing to Fianna Fáil. The Taoiseach did not take kindly to this. He insisted he'd worked hard to convince everyone from Unionists to US presidents that Sinn Féin was worth doing business with. He found it 'offensive' that so-called punishment beatings stopped when negotiations were in progress but resumed whenever talks stalled. 'I will give Sinn Féin full marks for discipline but for nothing else,' he snapped.

Commentators noted this was probably his strongest attack on Sinn Féin since the beginning of the peace process.

(26 January 2005)

MR. [CAOIMHGHÍN] Ó CAOLÁIN:	Everybody knows that we represent competing parties not only in respect of general elections but of all other electoral endeavours in this State. It has become ever more apparent that with the realisation that Sinn Féin presents a real and substantial challenge to the Taoiseach's party at the polls in this State, he has moved increasingly to what I see as a situation where he seeks to misrepresent Sinn Féin intent and tries to re-draw the contemporary history of the achievement of a new political dispensation on this island, the end of armed hostilities, the peace process and all that has flowed and has yet to flow from it.
	I do not believe for a moment that the Taoiseach's continual outbursts and allegations have anything to do with a bank robbery in Belfast but everything to do with votes in Ballybough and Ballyconnell and

everywhere else throughout this
jurisdiction.

MR. [WILLIE] O'DEA: Where is the Deputy's party getting
the money to buy those votes? It is
robbed money.

AN CEANN
COMHAIRLE [RORY
O'HANLON]:

Allow Deputy Ó Caoláin speak without interruption.

MR. Ó CAOLÁIN: With respect to the little whipper
at the Taoiseach's side, we never
interrupted you or any of the
participants—

MR. O'DEA: Robbed money.

AN CEANN
COMHAIRLE:

The Minister should allow Deputy Ó
Caoláin to speak.

MR. Ó CAOLÁIN: Deputy O'Dea would serve his position
and ministerial responsibilities better
if he learned to behave himself in this
House.

MR. [CONOR]
LENIHAN:

Is the Deputy threatening him?

MR. [DERMOT]
AHERN:

The veil is dropping.

(Interruptions.)

MR. O'DEA:	Robbed money.
AN CEANN COMHAIRLE:	The Chair has given some latitude with time to the other Members but Deputy Ó Caoláin is going well beyond the bounds of what is reasonable.
MR. Ó CAOLÁIN:	Does the Taoiseach not agree that in December we were closer to a comprehensive agreement than at any time previously? Does he accept and acknowledge that Sinn Féin, with the Irish Government and others, played a substantive part in the achievement of all that was to be delivered after 8 December?
	Does the Taoiseach recognise that a comprehensive agreement incorporated all the critical elements committed to by all the parties to the conflict and to the Good Friday Agreement negotiations? Does he not recognise this as the most important project for each and every one of us to address to ensure that we return, regroup and re-explore the potential to overcome the difficulties that presented themselves in the run-up to 8 December—
AN CEANN COMHAIRLE:	The Deputy should conclude as he has gone three minutes over time.

MR. Ó CAOLÁIN: —and to ensure that the peace process is back on track and the two Governments and all parties continue with their commitment to see its full realisation?

THE TAOISEACH: Deputy Ó Caoláin and all other Members can be certain that all of us will continue to do all the positive actions he has mentioned. We will do our very best because the people voted for the Good Friday Agreement. It is the policy of everybody in this House to continue to do that.

I understand why Deputy Ó Caoláin is looking around for an angle, which in this case is that the reasons are to do with party politics. If I had wished to fight his political party in a party political way, I certainly would not have done what I have been doing in recent years, such as doing everything possible to bring his party into the centre by ignoring all kinds of things and by trying to convince the DUP recently and the UUP for years of the benefits of working with Sinn Féin. I have tried to convince them of the security of doing so. I have tried to convince Presidents Bush and Clinton and President Prodi and others to put money into Northern Ireland to help peace and reconciliation. If I had only been interested in a political fight, I would not have taken those actions. Before we began taking those actions, the Deputy's party was a party with 2% support, but now it has a strong political mandate because people on all sides of this House, from the Labour Party to Fine Gael to Fianna Fáil to the Progressive Democrats to the Green Party, all worked to try to bring Sinn Féin in.

MR. Ó CAOLÁIN: Not at all.

THE TAOISEACH: We have done so because of our history.

The Deputy must understand that things must be equal. I refer to the kind of tactics in which some of his friends engage. In recent days a man was taken to a lay-by, shot in both hands and suffered a broken jaw. The reason for this assault is not known but it was carried out by the Provisional IRA. An 18 year old received gunshot wounds in both hands in an incident in Seaford Street in east Belfast, responsibility for which lies with the Provisional IRA. A punishment attack was carried out on a 19 year old man. He was shot in both hands and it is believed the Provisional IRA was responsible. The other day, a 19 year old man was shot in both ankles in an alley in Serbia Street, Lower Falls, and it is believed the Provisional IRA was responsible, and blah, blah, blah.

MR. Ó CAOLÁIN: It is blah, blah, blah.

(Interruptions.)

AN CEANN COMHAIRLE: Allow the Taoiseach speak without interruption, please.

THE TAOISEACH: I will fight Deputy Kenny's party. We will fight tough and hard politically. I will fight Deputy Rabbitte's party. However, it is very hard to fight that to which I have referred . . .

PART FOUR

Scandals

'Cough Up, the Party is
Looking for Money'

The Taoiseach insists he doesn't do business that way

This spat took place in January 1999 shortly after the then European Commissioner Padraig Flynn's infamous appearance on *The Late Late Show*. He had been quizzed about property developer Tom Gilmartin's allegation that in the late eighties he gave Mr. Flynn £50,000 intended for Fianna Fáil. Mr. Flynn told presenter Gay Byrne that he had never asked for or taken money from anybody for favours in his life. This, combined with the remarks he went on to make about Mr. Gilmartin's state of health, prompted Mr. Gilmartin to reconsider his decision not to co-operate with the Flood Tribunal.

The Taoiseach gave a statement saying he was certain he didn't ask Mr. Gilmartin for a contribution to Fianna Fáil or himself. 'It is not my way of doing business,' he said.

Questions from Opposition deputies followed, focusing on Mr. Ahern's memory of events. The Taoiseach admitted he had been surprised when he first heard the allegation about the £50,000.

'I was shocked that this amount of money could be floating around because it never floated anywhere that

I had been over the years.' For someone to take such a contribution would be inappropriate because it couldn't 'be explained to the ordinary man or woman in the street'.

(27 January 1999)

MR. [JOHN] BRUTON:

Mr. Tom Gilmartin says he met the Taoiseach when he attended a function in London, at which the Taoiseach was in attendance along with Mr. Flynn. He said he went to this meeting because he was under the impression it was a business meeting. He also says he left rather early because he discovered on arrival that it was a meeting at which people were being asked to give money to Fianna Fáil. The Taoiseach said he does not ask anybody for money and never has. Can he recollect from that meeting who broke the news to these invitees that they were not invited for the purpose of enlightenment but for financial reasons?

THE TAOISEACH [BERTIE AHERN]:

Deputy Bruton is trying to be rather witty—

MS. [MARIAN] McGENNIS:

He is not succeeding.

THE TAOISEACH:

—which perhaps helps the situation.

However, lest I am accused of not being clear, when I said I did not look for money I meant I was not part of the machine that could call somebody into the office and say 'cough up, the party is looking for money' or ring somebody up for the same purpose. I signed hundreds of letters—

MR. BRUTON: You will be telling us next you never asked for a vote.

MR. [MICHAEL] SMITH: He is good at that.

THE TAOISEACH: I can do that with some success. I probably wrote thousands of letters seeking money.

MR. SMITH: So has Deputy Bruton.

THE TAOISEACH: I am sure that, like Deputy Bruton in various places, I collected the odd few pound as well.

MR. BRUTON: It is being qualified all the time.

THE TAOISEACH: However, going out to ask for money is an entirely different matter.

Deputy Bruton is correct that a function was held by the party in England. It was a fund raising lunch. I do not have the details with me now but I had the date to hand a few days ago. These dates are in the party's records. The function in London was clearly a fund raising event and a number of Fianna Fáil people were at it. It was not a meeting and I do not know how anybody could have thought these functions were meetings. I do not know if Mr. Gilmartin was at it but if he says he was, I believe him. Pádraig Flynn, as treasurer, spoke at the function and other members of the party also attended.

MR. BRUTON: Could I ask—

AN LEAS-CHEANN COMHAIRLE [RORY O'HANLON]: I call Deputy Rabbitte. I will come back to Deputy Bruton.

MR. [PAT] RABBITTE: The Taoiseach did not comment in his statement about his views on the alleged attempts by Commissioner Flynn to influence Mr. Gilmartin as a witness to the tribunal and on the unpublished information, which I am sure is known to the Taoiseach, that Mr. Flynn importuned Mr. Gilmartin to meet him in England and said he would fly to England to see him, coincidentally in the same week the tribunal flew to England to see Mr. Gilmartin. What does the Taoiseach think about that?

If Mr. Seán Sherwin came forward now to say he had a memory of these times and events, why did he not come forward between 1989 and 1998 in respect of these matters? I had the pleasure of listening to the Taoiseach on 'Sunday Sport' during the Christmas recess. Over at least one hour he rivalled Jimmy Magee with his memory of great events that happened in Dalymount Park in the 1960s and in Croke Park in the 1970s.

MR. [DERMOT] AHERN:	This is becoming a farce.
MR. RABBITTE:	Can the Taoiseach give a plausible explanation as to why he cannot remember somebody who came to him in the late 1980s with a project worth £500 million? Is there a plausible explanation as to why this should slip his mind?
MR. [BRIAN]COWEN:	It is hard to take lectures on selective amnesia from Democratic Left.

(Interruptions.)

MR. RABBITTE:	Does the Taoiseach recall what answer he gave to question No. 22 of the tribunal's questionnaire? It

required us to state whether we were aware of any payment or offer to any public representative in respect of tax designation or the provision of services, including roads, to any property in the State.

THE TAOISEACH:

There are four questions dealing with influencing tribunal witnesses. I do not know if that happens, therefore I did not include it in my speech. If tribunal witnesses were interfered with, it is entirely wrong and inappropriate and legally wrong as in any other case.

I do not know whether these matters jogged Seán Sherwin's mind when he saw them. At least he made a statement. That statement which has been given to the tribunal is there and the tribunal has interviewed him. That is to his credit. He could have perhaps made it before, but he has now given it to the appropriate tribunal.

In relation to the £500 million project, while I have a good memory on the matter of All-Ireland finals and sport quizzes generally, and have a good recollection normally, I do not remember every single meeting. Incidentally when going back over the diaries, they included people whom I met a number of times but could not recall them. In one such case I checked the reason I met a trade union on so many occasions at a particular time. It was because it was amalgamating. I had met the trade union about ten times in that period and I did not recall it. When one meets a large number of people it is impossible to recall them all.

I remember the meeting with Mr. Gilmartin, as I said to Deputy Bruton earlier, because it was such a big project in a run-down part of my constituency. The others were follow on meetings. I did not say they did not take place and I am not arguing about that.

In regard to Question No. 22, I am sure the answer I gave was 'no information', for the same reason I gave earlier that I would not state something I could not stand over, but I will give details and information to the tribunal.

As Leader of Fianna Fáil and as Uachtarán Fianna Fáil to the extent of being boring to my colleagues, I have done my utmost to tidy up a situation, not where anybody has done anything wrong but to ensure for the future that we operate in as transparent a manner as possible because that is the way society is today. I will continue to do that and I am glad of their support for that in recent years.

MR. RABBITTE: After the Taoiseach became treasurer, did he ever put any questions to his colleagues about the alleged practice of moneys donated to the party not reaching the party?

DEPUTIES: Did the Deputy?

MR. RABBITTE: In respect of the answer to Question No. 22, did the Taoiseach say 'no' that he did not know of any payment to any public representative in respect of any development to do with any property in the State? The answer in the questionnaire is 'yes' or 'no'.

THE TAOISEACH: I assume I did, subject to checking it.

MR. RABBITTE: I would like to hear it on the record of the House.

THE TAOISEACH: If Deputy Rabbitte is asking me when filling up my form if I was aware of anyone who had in a fraudulent or corrupt way received money for any development, I am sure I would have answered 'no' because I would not have any evidence of that.

MR. RABBITTE: Did you answer 'yes' or 'no'? I take it the record shows the Taoiseach is saying 'no'.

MR. BRUTON: Is the Taoiseach aware of any meetings organised by Fianna Fáil with groups of builders to discuss strategy for development generally, including tax designation, during the early 1990s?

THE TAOISEACH: Fianna Fáil would have strategy meetings with many sectors, not just builders, trying to promote employment, agriculture and tourism but not on the basis of deciding strategy for tax designation. If the implication is whether these people would have an influence on these matters, the answer is 'no'.

MR. BRUTON: No meetings took place to discuss tax designation with groups of builders.

THE TAOISEACH: Not to my knowledge.

MR. BRUTON: The Taoiseach said last night he regarded some contributions made to parties and politicians as appropriate and others as inappropriate. From what he knows about it, does the Taoiseach think the contribution made by Mr. Gilmartin to Mr. Flynn was appropriate or inappropriate?

THE TAOISEACH:	I have no information on whether the contribution was actually given but as I have said previously in this House if people take contributions of £30,000, £40,000 or £50,000 it is very hard to explain and for that reason I do not think people should do that. Contributions of that order cannot ever be explained to the ordinary man or woman in the street. For that reason I do not think they are appropriate.
MR. BRUTON:	Was the Taoiseach shocked when he heard of this allegation?
THE TAOISEACH:	Yes.
MR. BRUTON:	Given that the Taoiseach was shocked about this allegation did he not confide in the Tánaiste?
THE TAOISEACH:	I told my programme manager to inform the Tánaiste's programme manager that any matters related to the articles in the newspapers were being dealt with in the legal way.
MR. BRUTON:	While the Taoiseach is very important and busy—
A DEPUTY:	So too is the Deputy.
MR. BRUTON:	—it would appear when it comes to

asking Pádraig Flynn about money that belongs to Fianna Fáil, he does not ask him directly but lets somebody else do it. Why does he not like to ask him face to face? When it comes to telling the Tánaiste about something which the Taoiseach admits has shocked him—most people agree the Tánaiste is probably his closest and certainly his most important colleague in Government and they have a close working relationship—is it not surprising he did not even tell the Tánaiste of this knowledge and that he let her find out about it in the newspapers?

THE TAOISEACH: When Deputy Bruton went to collect £50,000 he did not know his colleague had been there to collect £30,000 a short time earlier.

(Interruptions.)

THE TAOISEACH: I was shocked that this amount of money could be floating around because it never floated anywhere that I had been over the years. It is inappropriate. The Tánaiste runs her party and I do my utmost with my colleagues to run our party. What I did was to make sure that matters which had to do with Mr. Sherwin and the tribunal were in the tribunal where they would be properly investigated. Regarding the insinuation that instead of being down in the office discussing European matters I should be chasing Mr. Flynn about what he may have done in 1989, it would be inappropriate to do that. I put the letter and the facts on record.

The general secretary on behalf of the trustees wrote concerning the matter, our officials went to the tribunal and gave all the evidence to it and it will be investigated. That was the right thing to do. The tribunal also has the affidavit of Mr. Gilmartin. That is entirely the correct way to proceed and was the way I was advised to proceed by the Fianna Fáil legal team.

MR. QUINN:

Does the Taoiseach agree that these matters are being discussed here today because Mr. Flynn gave an interview on *The Late Late Show* some weeks ago which provoked Mr. Gilmartin into making a series of allegations?

The Taoiseach and Deputy Lawlor have categorically denied one of the allegations made by Mr. Gilmartin in respect of a meeting with himself, Mr. Haughey, Mr. Flynn, the late Deputy Lenihan and Deputy Lawlor. I accept the stated position as of now is that there is a conflict in that the Members of this House who are present now—the Taoiseach and Deputy Lawlor—have categorically denied that such a meeting took place and, to whit, the Taoiseach has no record or recollection of such a meeting. I agree that such a meeting with so many Ministers in attendance would have left a record somewhere.

I have two questions arising from that observation. Will the search for records continue after today, because this matter has come upon all of us quickly? Do I take it that the Tánaiste's qualified support for the Government remains qualified or has there been a change in that? If she had taken the five minutes available to her, she might have been able to speak for herself, unless she wishes to speak now through the Chair. Do I take it that the support remains qualified?

On a question of judgment rather than of fact, and the Taoiseach may not want to answer it but why does he think Mr. Gilmartin is making these very serious allegations?

THE TAOISEACH: I assure the House and Deputy Quinn that we will continue to check the records because these are important matters. Today more of these letters and minutes were found. I am sure further trawls will find more because they will be subject to the tribunals anyway. If I come across anything which indicates I have misled this House, I will do what I have continually done: I will publicly inform the House.

Even though this matter is appropriate for the tribunal, the events of recent days bring it in here. I saw a note today that Mr. Gilmartin made these statements because of remarks which were made on *The Late Late Show*. I believe what he has said and I know of no other reasons for these allegations. Mr. Gilmartin, from my memory of him was a respected developer working in some capacity for Ireland and had made a great deal of money in Britain. He is a Sligo person by birth. He was involved in two big projects—one of which was the Bachelor's Walk project which was not completed because only 60 per cent of the land was acquired before it was taken over by another company which changed its plans and made decisions in Dublin. I do not know all the details of Quarryvale although I have read much about it. That did not work either so I am sure there is a certain level of dissatisfaction that neither of these developments worked.

MR. BRUTON:

Did the Taoiseach see a copy of the letter which the general secretary of Fianna Fáil sent to Mr. Pádraig Flynn before it was sent and did he approve the text? Did he think it appropriate that the general secretary should say to Mr. Flynn that he regretted any inconvenience he might cause to Mr. Flynn in dealing with the query and that no doubt he would appreciate the legal necessity for this line of inquiry.

MR. COWEN:

The Deputy is fishing without a rod.

THE 'HEADS IN BASKETS'
APPROACH TO POLITICS

Denis Foley's departure

In February 2000, the Taoiseach Bertie Ahern said Denis Foley was now effectively an Independent TD, having resigned from the Fianna Fáil parliamentary party after it emerged that he had been called before the Moriarty Tribunal to explain his financial affairs. It had been an embarrassing situation for the Government, given that Mr. Foley had been vice-chairman of the Public Accounts Committee at the time. Mr. Ahern admitted it was 'deeply disappointing' to discover that Mr. Foley had been 'conducting his financial affairs in a manner analogous to that being investigated by the sub-committee'.

But he criticised members of the House whose 'heads in baskets' approach to politics meant they constantly called for instant political executions. And when Opposition deputies complained that he wasn't answering their questions, he hit out at Fine Gael TDs by reminding them of Michael Lowry's comment to John Bruton as he left that party under a cloud, 'My very best friend—do you remember that one? My very, very best friend forever.'

(09 February 2000)

THE TAOISEACH
[BERTIE AHERN]:

I was gravely disappointed to learn that a member of my own party in this House would be called to give evidence to the Moriarty tribunal. My disappointment deepened on learning that he had over a long period evaded his responsibility as a citizen to observe and fulfil his obligations under the tax code.

The first inkling I had of the possible involvement of Deputy Foley in the Moriarty tribunal was from the Government Press Secretary, who was picking up a report circulating among journalists. This was in early December. I subsequently checked the Ansbacher list that had been furnished to me, but found that Deputy Foley's name was not on it. I next had a report to the same effect from the Attorney General. He had been informed by the Tánaiste, who had learnt from her officer, Gerard Ryan, that Deputy Foley was likely to be called before the Moriarty tribunal. At that time, the Public Accounts Committee sub-committee's hearings were complete, and the publication of their report was believed to be imminent.

On Wednesday 15 December, the day before the House went into recess for the Christmas period, I asked Deputy Foley to come to see me so that I might question him about the matter. I wish to emphasise that I always regard such conversations with Deputies in my party as strictly confidential.

However, given the circumstances involved, I will convey the essential and most relevant points to the House. It was a fairly short meeting. He admitted to me that he had been before the Moriarty tribunal in private session and that he was co-operating fully with the tribunal. I asked him what it was about, because he was not on the Ansbacher list that I had. He said it related to investments going back 26 or 28 years when he was involved in the hotel near his house in Tralee and not a Deputy at the time. He informed me that the accountant who then did work for the hotel was Des Traynor and that he was putting money that he was getting through this business into an investment account with Mr. Traynor.

I reminded him that it was Fianna Fáil policy to co-operate fully with tribunals. I told him that the co-operation was essential and that total and full disclosure was critical. He assured me that he had already done that and would continue to do so. Deputy Foley also told me that he had been with his accountant and that they were in the process of making a full and voluntary disclosure to the Revenue Commissioners, with a view to settling his liabilities. I asked him whether he had considered his position on the Committee of Public Accounts. The DIRT sub-committee's work had finished, and its report had been published that day. He informed me that he would resign from the committee. He said that he would do this at the earliest appropriate opportunity, which he thought would be prior to his scheduled public appearance at the tribunal, which was due early on the tribunal's resumption after the Christmas break.

Deputy Foley has since stated that he believed, until recently, that his offshore account did not create a conflict of interest, vis-à-vis either his membership of the Committee of Public Accounts or the DIRT inquiry. This view failed to exercise the political judgment that would be expected of him after long years in this House. The Tánaiste and I discussed the fact that Deputy Foley was facing difficulties and was to appear before the Moriarty tribunal. We did not have any detailed discussion on the matter because we both respect her statutory role in relation to the investigation of the Ansbacher and related accounts. As reported in newspapers recently, I informed the Tánaiste that I had spoken to Deputy Foley and that he had assured me that he intended to resign from the PAC.

MR. [RÚAIRÍ] QUINN: Will the Taoiseach yield for a question?

THE TAOISEACH: No, I will not yield for a question. I came in here to answer questions about private conversations which I should not be answering.

MR. QUINN: Did the Taoiseach ask Deputy Foley if he had an Ansbacher account?

AN LEAS-CHEANN COMHAIRLE [RORY O'HANLON]: The Taoiseach has intimated he wishes to continue.

THE TAOISEACH: It is in my script—he told me the type of account he had.

MS. [RÓISÍN] SHORTALL: Did the Taoiseach ask him?

THE TAOISEACH: He told me.

MRS. [NORA] OWEN: Did the Taoiseach ask him?

AN LEAS-CHEANN COMHAIRLE:	The Taoiseach, without interruption.

THE TAOISEACH: As always, a Leas-Cheann Comhairle, the do-gooders in the Labour Party do not want to hear the facts. Deputy Foley's conduct is now a matter for the tribunal and for a number of other authorities. I am aware that his conduct is also being brought before the Committee on Procedure and Privileges of this House.

MR. QUINN: The most cunning, the most devious—

THE TAOISEACH: That is the Deputy. On foot of a formal complaint from Deputy Quinn, the Committee on Members' Interests—

MRS. OWEN: The mask is slipping.

THE TAOISEACH: —which is a statutory committee under the Ethics in Public Office Act, 1995, will decide in a formal investigation on Deputy Foley's position and will report to this House without delay as required by the Act.

On a previous occasion in this House, in the case of another Deputy who admitted to having an offshore account and evading tax, the then Taoiseach, Deputy John Bruton, said on 3 December 1996, Dáil Official Report, volume 472, column 463, that nobody is above the law and that:

There is not, and never will be, a system of conviction by denunciation. Independent authorities, not rivals nor those with an axe to grind, made judgments as to culpability.

All of us in this House are concerned about the standing of politics. I have on many occasions over the past three years, and from both sides of the House, set out my views on what constitutes acceptable standards for a public representative. I have stressed the fundamental issue of public trust and above all our duty to respect the rules which we ourselves legislate for. The work of the Committee of Public Accounts and its report on the operation of DIRT tax have been highly praised on all sides. It is, apart from any other consideration, deeply disappointing to find that a Member of the House, and a vice-chairman and past chairman of the Public Account Committee, was prima facie conducting his financial affairs in a manner analogous to that being investigated by the sub-committee.

In light of these circumstances, Deputy Foley has properly informed me of his resignation from the Fianna

Fáil Parliamentary Party. He has also today informed me of his decision not to contest the elections to the Fianna Fáil National Executive. He is now, in effect, an Independent TD.

MR. [P.J.] SHEEHAN

He is better off now than he was before.

THE TAOISEACH:

I think we should also acknowledge the very full and sincere apology that he made at the tribunal yesterday to his family, colleagues and constituents. In fairness to Deputy Foley, his is the first apology of its kind that has been heard from anyone involved in any of the tribunals.

MR. QUINN:

We are still waiting for Charlie's.

THE TAOISEACH:

I applaud his courage and decency in that regard. We have to make it clear that certain behaviour from any quarter is completely unacceptable. The Fianna Fáil Parliamentary Party this morning approved a code of conduct, which will be submitted first to the National Executive and then to the Fianna Fáil Ard-Fheis early next month—

MS. SHORTALL:

That is a joke.

THE TAOISEACH:	The Labour Party should have one.
AN LEAS-CHEANN COMHAIRLE:	The Taoiseach without interruption.
MRS. [MARY] O'ROURKE:	Have they heard of Woodchester?
THE TAOISEACH:	It will come into effect immediately after the Fianna Fáil Ard-Fheis. It covers the requirement that all relevant interests must be declared, and that public representatives must act at all times with honesty and integrity. Anyone standing for election must be able to confirm that their tax affairs are either in order or being finally put in order. I wish to point out that Fianna Fáil is the first and, thus far, the only political party in this House to take such an initiative.
MRS. OWEN:	They promised it in 1997.
MR. [SÉAN] RYAN:	There is no need for it here.
	(Interruptions.)
AN LEAS-CHEANN COMHAIRLE:	Members should allow the Taoiseach to continue.
THE TAOISEACH:	Legislation to establish an ethics

commission will be brought before this House later this year.

(Interruptions.)

AN LEAS-CHEANN COMHAIRLE:	Silence please; allow the Taoiseach to continue without interruption.

THE TAOISEACH: Other than clearer rules, and the deterrent of an adverse effect on both reputation and personal finances if they are flouted, there is no early warning system that can be put in place to alert us to problems of this kind. These situations can exist for some time before they are brought to anyone's attention. I am satisfied in this case that the correct and proportionate action has been taken without any undue delay.

There are those in this House who have a 'heads in baskets' approach to politics and who are always urging instant political executions—

MR. QUINN: Ask Albert.

THE TAOISEACH: —without allowing any time for consideration, reflection or adjustment.

MRS. OWEN: There is a touch of Marie Antoinette —heads in baskets and guillotines.

AN LEAS-CHEANN COMHAIRLE:	Opposition Members will have an opportunity to speak without interruption.
THE TAOISEACH:	It is almost pointless coming to this House to answer questions because no one ever wants to listen.
MRS. OWEN:	The Taoiseach is not answering the questions.
MR. [NOEL] DEMPSEY:	Every one of them were answered.
THE TAOISEACH:	Every one of them.
MRS. OWEN:	No dates.
THE TAOISEACH:	I have given the dates. Does it hurt?
MRS. OWEN:	When was the first inkling? When did the Attorney General and the Tánaiste speak to the Taoiseach?
AN LEAS-CHEANN COMHAIRLE:	I ask Deputy Owen to allow the Taoiseach to continue without interruption. He is entitled to that courtesy, as is any other Member of the House.
THE TAOISEACH:	A Leas-Cheann Comhairle, I am comprehensively answering all the questions listed.

Mr. Quinn: He is not.

The Taoiseach: If the Labour Party has thought of other questions—

    (Interruptions.)

The Taoiseach: The questions were listed and I am answering them.

Mr. [Andrew] Boylan: Does the Taoiseach want to phone a friend?

The Taoiseach: My very best friend—do you remember that one? My very, very best friend forever.

    (Interruptions.)

The Taoiseach: Fine Gael still did not establish a code of conduct. It still did not introduce any party rules about taxes.

An Leas-Cheann Comhairle: Will the Taoiseach please address his remarks through the chair?

The Taoiseach: Where are the Fine Gael rules on tax policy? It had to throw one of its members out, even though a tribunal was set up especially for him.

Mrs. Owen: He left the party.

MRS. O'ROURKE: He was a long time in that Department.

THE TAOISEACH: I am second to no one in my concern to see the right thing happen but I believe that where action is required it should be consistent with the public interest, be done in a humane way, with some compassion for the feelings of the individuals concerned who find themselves in a difficult and humiliating personal situation, and for their family.

It is better from every point of view if the individual can be brought to understand the action that is required, and that they acknowledge the justice of it, by taking the necessary steps themselves. On occasion, a little space may need to be given.

I do not consider that in this instance the public interest suffered in any way by the short delay that occurred over the Christmas recess. It has been beneficial that many of the questions raised by Deputy Foley's conduct could be put to him as soon as possible thereafter in the tribunal, even if not all questions have necessarily received completely satisfactory answers. I believe that the proper course of action would have been for

Deputy Foley to absent himself from membership of the DIRT committee altogether.

Members of this House, and those who aspire to take part in political life, will, I hope, have taken note once again of the high standards expected of those in public life, which the Government has shown a determination to uphold. Seamus Heaney's new translation of Beowulf contains the lines, 'Behaviour that's admired is the path to power among people everywhere'. We need hardly remind ourselves that the converse is especially true in a democracy.

'THE JACKBOOT TENDENCY'

Conor Lenihan revives Civil War politics

This debate on the Prevention of Corruption Bill followed days of sensational evidence concerning Liam Lawlor at the Flood Tribunal in December 2000. In the Dáil, Fine Gael's Alan Shatter accused Fianna Fáil of tolerating the behaviour of Mr. Lawlor (who had resigned from the party earlier in the year). While insisting that his own party should not be associated with what was 'seeping from the Fianna Fáil benches', he goaded Conor Lenihan. 'Tell us about Deputy Lawlor and the Government that depends on him.'

Mr. Lenihan dismissed this as a typical Fine Gael approach. His colourful description of the party's 'brief dalliance with fascism in the 1930s' prompted Mr. Shatter to suggest, 'The Deputy should take a full stand-up comedy routine in the Gaiety Theatre. He should join Equity.'

(15 December 2000)

MR. [CONOR] LENIHAN:	The party he takes pride in tried to promulgate fascism in Ireland in [the]1930s, trying to tilt us towards the jackboot tendency then in Europe. That is what it is at today also; it is the usual Fine Gael jackboot tendency, trying to tar Fianna Fáil and all its members with one brush. We have problems and we are the first to acknowledge that. The Taoiseach, the Minister for Justice, Equality and Law Reform and all my parliamentary colleagues have been to the fore in ensuring that higher standards apply. We will have been four years in office next June and every time there is a hue and cry from Deputies opposite about standards and ethics and the need for greater compliance with the tax code or the standards of the House we have been first to act. We were the first to bring forward legislation. We were the first to raise the bar and we were the first to call for the tribunals; we called for those when in Opposition. If Deputy Shatter examines his party leader's record—
MR. [ALAN] SHATTER:	The Deputy must be joking.
MR. C. LENIHAN:	—he was tardy in moving on some of his colleagues who had transgressed on the ethical code. Unusually,

Deputy Bruton was more than quick to forgive during the Tipperary South by-election and to apply the principles of Christianity to one Member who made a serious transgression and who is the subject of serious investigation in a public tribunal. He was quick to forgive—the 'best friends forever' factor is still at play in Fine Gael. At least when we move against our own we do so clearly and insist on compliance. The record is there.

MR. SHATTER: They keep on voting with Fianna Fáil, they stay in Fianna Fáil offices and remain as vice-chairmen of committees Fianna Fáil control. That is a vigorous move against corrupt members of Fianna Fáil. Some of them—

MR. C. LENIHAN: I am glad the Deputy has interrupted.

ACTING CHAIRMAN: I ask both Deputies to try to respect the Chamber in which they are and to address comments through the Chair. Will Deputy Lenihan continue his speech?

MR. SHATTER: I am being provoked.

MR. C. LENIHAN: I would love to. I welcome Deputy Shatter's intervention regarding the vice-chairman of the Committee on Finance and the Public Services. Deputy Shatter will know that the committees are decided on a pro rata basis and shared among different parties. Deputy Lawlor, in turn and in time-honoured fashion, was appointed vice-chairman and that is a matter for the committee to resolve. It was strange that Deputy Deenihan was flying with the usually active Fine Gael fax machine, faxing to the committee secretariat at 10.20 a.m. this morning his anger and worry that Deputy Lawlor should be on the committee.

MR. SHATTER: The Taoiseach has no say in who is appointed.

MR. C. LENIHAN: Where was Fine Gael months ago when Deputy Lawlor was the subject of inquiry and controversy? It has become a rather late convert to the idea that he is an inappropriate person to sit on that committee. Several months ago Deputy Lawlor might be said to have been in greater controversy when under investigation by his own party—

MR. SHATTER: He had not committed perjury at that time.

MR. C. LENIHAN: —and forced, in some manner or fashion, to resign not only from the parliamentary party but the party itself. After he ceased to be a member of Fianna Fáil by his own choice I never heard from any Fine Gael representative either on that committee, in the Dáil or at the leadership level, represented by Deputy Bruton, call for his resignation as vice-chairman of the committee. This is rank hypocrisy of the kind we see played out every day here on matters of ethics in public life.

Fine Gael is no rose when it comes to ethics and compliance. We know about the debt Fine Gael cleared when it came into Government in 1994 by some form of democratic coup perpetrated against the then Taoiseach, Deputy Albert Reynolds, in which, against the public interest and mood, Fine Gael was pushed into power with no support or mandate from the people. It was foisted on the Irish people and into power. It quickly broke up the peace process, but we have never heard Fine Gael properly explain how it managed magically over two years to wipe out a debt of some £6 million because of the very successful fund-raising techniques applied by a person who is no longer apparently a member of that party but is quite prominent when it comes to christianity and forgiveness, when christianity is spoken about on the Opposition benches. I find it amusing that has never been explained.

Also, when it comes to ethics and how business people interact with Government, it is important there is a proper measured response when dealing with business. Business has a right to lobby Government and to interact with Ministers and Deputies and tell them what they would like in an ideal world. However, it seems odd that when Fine Gael was fundraising, and raising money from one Ben Dunne, it did not just look for a donation, but after dinner when the cigars were produced and the coffee was poured, it rather generously and gladheartedly asked Mr. Ben Dunne—and this is on public record—whether, now that he had coughed up the cash, there were any policies he would like to influence that Fine Gael could put forward on this behalf? That is the kind of craven approach taken by Fine Gael when it comes to raising money from big capital holders and money men. It immediately invites them to write its party policy. One would not find that in Fianna Fáil. Probably one of the greatest complaints that businessmen make about Fianna Fáil is that we take the money and donations, run the race days and the golf events and they do not receive anything in return. That is politics. We are a more robust party than Fine Gael.

MR. SHATTER:

There are a great many millionaires attached to Fianna Fáil.

MR. C. LENIHAN:

We are more used to dealing with power, sometimes as a majority party, whereas the party opposite seldom gets into power, and when it does, it has to hang up the white flag when it comes to policy because the left wingers always win when Fine Gael is in power.

MR. SHATTER:

The Deputy is a political Alice in Wonderland type character. He will bring the rabbit into the story next.

MR. C. LENIHAN:

No robust right-wing Fine Gael Government has been elected since 1973. Even Liam Cosgrave, the elder, found it difficult to deal with the Labour incubus once it was brought into his ranks. It was a less than right-wing robust Fine Gael Government.

It shouts and talks a great deal in Opposition but when it gets into Government, it is the parties of the left and the Labour Party that tend to influence policy.

The Bill before the House represents firm action, but action informed by a sense of proportion and perspective to deal with the problem of corruption. The Bill is welcome in itself but also for recognising that corruption is an international and not simply an Irish problem. The ratification of international conventions shows that Ireland is fully prepared to play its part in the fight against this subversive menace to democracy. International corruption has been compounded and exacerbated by the fall of the Iron Curtain and the demise of the Soviet Union. Deputy Shatter, who has travelled a lot, will know a great deal about the morals and ethics that applied in countries other than Ireland.

MR. SHATTER:

It seems Deputy Lawlor is more acquainted with Eastern Europe than most of us are at this stage.

MR. C. LENIHAN:

I suppose I should be loathe to quote a former leader of my party, but what happens here is in the ha'penny place compared with what occurs in other jurisdictions. I had the pleasure of working in the newly liberated countries of the eastern bloc, particularly the Czech Republic, Hungary and Poland, where the levels of corruption are quite horrifying, mainly due to the low pay that public administrators and officials receive in those countries.

MR. SHATTER: I am surprised Deputy Lawlor did not consult the Deputy about the Czech Republic.

MR. C. LENIHAN: For example, a secretary of a department circa 1992 in the Czech Republic would earn something in the order of $300 a month and, therefore, the temptations are huge, when international capital and business is invested in that country, to spread that money around to influence those public officials by giving them bribes. This is a huge phenomenon in the eastern bloc and in those countries that were formerly communist in origin. The great irony, which Deputy Shatter will appreciate, coming as he does from a robust right wing party like Fine Gael—

MR. SHATTER: The Deputy should take a full stand-

up comedy routine in the Gaiety
Theatre. He should join Equity.

'THE YOUNG GENERATION'

John Deasy gets shown the door

Before he was sacked from the Fine Gael front bench for smoking in the Dáil bar, John Deasy was already proving to be a rebel by getting himself thrown out of the chamber by the Ceann Comhairle in October 2002. Mr. Deasy was objecting to the Taoiseach's refusal to answer questions on the Flood Report. His party leader Enda Kenny called him 'a representative of the younger generation, appalled at what's going on here'.

(09 October 2002)

MR. [JOHN] DEASY:	The Taoiseach is making the House irrelevant.
AN CEANN COMHAIRLE [RORY O'HANLON]:	That does not arise. I call Deputy Gormley.
MR. DEASY:	There is no point in being in the House.

AN CEANN COMHAIRLE:	Deputy Deasy should resume his seat.
MR. DEASY:	There is no point in being here anymore.
AN CEANN COMHAIRLE:	I have called Deputy Gormley on the European Union (Scrutiny) Bill.
MR. DEASY:	Why will the Taoiseach not answer questions?
AN CEANN COMHAIRLE:	I have called Deputy Gormley. Deputy Deasy is out of order.
MR. DEASY:	Of what is the Taoiseach afraid?
AN CEANN COMHAIRLE:	Deputy Deasy should resume his seat.
MR. DEASY:	The Taoiseach is making the Chamber irrelevant.
AN CEANN COMHAIRLE:	The Deputy should resume his seat because he is out of order.
MR. DEASY:	No I will not.
AN CEANN COMHAIRLE:	If the Deputy does not do so, he will have to leave the House. He should resume his seat.

MR. DEASY:	There is no point being in the House.
AN CEANN COMHAIRLE:	The Deputy should resume his seat. If he does not, he should leave the House. Does he wish to leave the House?
MR. DEASY:	There is no point in being here.
MR. [BRIAN] LENIHAN:	He should resign his seat in that case.
AN CEANN COMHAIRLE:	Deputy Deasy must leave the House.
MR. [BERNARD] DURKAN:	A Cheann Comhairle—
AN CEANN COMHAIRLE:	Deputy Deasy had an opportunity to resume his seat.
MR. DURKAN:	A Cheann Comhairle—
AN CEANN COMHAIRLE:	We are dealing with a matter, Deputy.
MR. DURKAN:	I am aware of that. I appeal to the Ceann Comhairle—
AN CEANN COMHAIRLE:	I propose that Deputy Deasy leave the House.
MR. DURKAN:	—in the interests of transparency and fair play—

AN CEANN COMHAIRLE:	I have already decided on the matter.
MR. [ENDA] KENNY:	He is one of the young generation and he is appalled by what he has seen.
AN CEANN COMHAIRLE:	If Members obeyed the Chair, they might not be so appalled.
	(Interruptions.)
AN CEANN COMHAIRLE:	Deputy Deasy must leave the House.

If I knew Then What I know Now

The Flood Report finds Ray Burke corrupt

ine Gael's Gay Mitchell described the findings of the Flood Tribunal's second interim report, released in September 2002, as 'the greatest scandal since the Arms Trial'. Ray Burke—appointed Minister for Foreign Affairs by Bertie Ahern five years previously—was found to have acted corruptly. Mr. Justice Fergus Flood ruled that Mr. Burke had received corrupt payments from builders and that he had taken decisions not in the public interest after receiving money on behalf of Century Radio.

'Rambo' had resigned from the Government and Dáil in October 1997 and at that time the Taoiseach had bemoaned the Opposition's 'persistant hounding of an honourable man'. But during this debate in October 2002, Mr. Ahern came under pressure to explain why he had brought Mr. Burke back into the Cabinet in September 1997 while a cloud of suspicion hung over him. The Taoiseach said the decision was based on his own inquiries, as well as Mr. Burke's political abilities and assurances that he had done nothing wrong. 'I took the man's word,' he said.

(09 October 2002)

THE TAOISEACH [BERTIE AHERN]:	. . . I have been criticised again today for appointing Ray Burke to Cabinet in 1997. Given the information revealed by Justice Flood, the judgment of hindsight is very clear. However, one's judgment at any given time is formed on the basis of what one believes is true at the time and the evidence then available. Of course I would not have appointed Ray Burke to Cabinet if I knew what I know now, five years later.
MR. [JIM] O'KEEFFE:	Did the Taoiseach want to know?
THE TAOISEACH:	My decision at the time was a bona fide one based on Mr. Burke's undisputed political abilities, his categorical assurance he had done nothing wrong and a number of inquiries. In my speech to the House tomorrow I intend to outline the investigation carried out in respect of rumours and allegations concerning the payment of money in relation to planning matters—most of these issues are already on the Dáil record.

In reply to Deputy Kenny, it is sufficient to say that I was misled by Ray Burke, as was this House. Since the interim report of the Flood tribunal was published I have made my position clear. I condemn the corrupt activities and I have expressed my sense of betrayal. The obvious reason why anyone is appointed to a position is because of their competence and ability to do the job.

I refer Deputies to what I told the House on 3 June 1998 when I stated: The first question I am asked is why I appointed Mr. Burke Minister for Foreign Affairs last June. Mr. Burke was an experienced and capable Minister, who had participated in an earlier phase of the talks process and in the work of the Anglo-Irish Inter-governmental Conference As Leader of the Opposition, I had worked very well with him on Northern Ireland and European matters, where his judgment was very good. He was eminently qualified for the job of Minister for Foreign Affairs. When we came into office, I remind Deputies that there was no renewed IRA ceasefire and the talks had been stalled and going nowhere for over 12 months. Even in the short time that he was Minister he made his mark and we had arrived at a situation by the end of September where both the Ulster Unionists and Sinn Féin were sitting around the same table with others within weeks of a new IRA ceasefire.

In reply to Deputy Howlin, I made

my decision to appoint Ray Burke on the basis of the information that was available to me then—

MR. [TOMMY] BROUGHAN: The Taoiseach knew he was misleading the House.

THE TAOISEACH: —and the repeated assurance to me. The fact that I called Ray Burke an honourable man underlines the fact that I genuinely believed the assurance he had given me when I questioned him.

MS. [OLIVIA] MITCHELL: It shows very poor judgment at best.

THE TAOISEACH: In other situations others have taken colleagues at their word. On 3 December 1996, in a debate on the resignation of Michael Lowry, Deputy Kenny stated:

I very much regret the departure of Deputy Michael Lowry from Cabinet. I have known him for many years both as a member of Fine Gael and as a Government colleague and he is a man of the highest integrity and honour.

The then Tánaiste, former Deputy Spring, stated, 'I have no difficulty in accepting Deputy Lowry's assertion of integrity and propriety.' Hindsight is not foresight. What I know now is a different situation to what I knew then.

MR. KENNY:

Does the Taoiseach now admit that the questions he asked in respect of the appointment of Raphael Burke to the Cabinet were adequate? Does he admit that he knew that Mr. Burke had received a £30,000 payment? Will he tell the House what information was given to him by former Taoiseach, Mr. Albert Reynolds, before he made that appointment? Will he tell the House what information was given to him by the then Minister for the Environment, Deputy Michael Smith, when he carried out an investigation on this matter? What oral or written evidence was given to him by the former Minister for Justice, Máire Geoghegan-Quinn, before he made that appointment? The Tánaiste had received information from the present Minister for Justice, Equality and Law Reform, Deputy McDowell, that these matters were contradictory. Did he not think it fit and appropriate that he should speak to people like Mr. Bailey, Mr. Brennan, Mr. McGowan or, indeed, Mr. Gogarty, the person making the most allegations. With the whiff and the rumour and the swirling doubts that surrounded Ray Burke, it should have been perfectly obvious to the Taoiseach that here was a man who was legitimately held in deep suspicion by the public. As such this was a person not fit to hold high office and the Taoiseach's judgment in appointing him was flawed.

THE TAOISEACH: If all those things were said at that time we would not have had a debate in this House on the night the Government was appointed. Not one Member of this House—

MS. MITCHELL: We did not know what the Taoiseach knew.

MR. GAY MITCHELL: Máire Geoghegan-Quinn did not tell us.

MR. RABBITTE: The Taoiseach ought to know. That is all raiméis.

AN CEANN COMHAIRLE [RORY O'HANLON]: I request Members to allow the Taoiseach the same courtesy that was offered to Deputy Kenny. The Taoiseach is entitled to be heard in silence in this House. I ask the Deputy to resume his seat. This is Leaders' questions, Deputy Rabbitte. The Deputy is not the leader yet. I ask him to obey the Standing Orders of the House.

THE TAOISEACH: May I remind Deputy Rabbitte of two famous occasions in this House when people stood up. Some famous speeches have been made in this House.

MR. RABBITTE: I was not one of those people.

THE TAOISEACH: I did not say that the Deputy was one of those people.

MR. [MICHAEL] RING: Those people were right.

THE TAOISEACH: It was not the convention for people to get up and speak. I wish to answer the questions asked by the Deputies. I made whatever investigations I could. They are all documented in the record and I will outline them again tomorrow. Deputy Smith's inquiry in 1993 did not result in any facts or evidence being given to me. In December 1994, Máire Geoghegan-Quinn gave me a report and, as a result, the Mahfouz file was examined by the Minister who took over in the Department of Justice, former Deputy Nora Owen. I was out of office for a period of two and a half years. When I came back into office the tribunals had been set up. All those files are now subject to investigation by the Moriarty tribunal.

I received a memo from the then Minister, Máire Geoghegan-Quinn, prior to my leaving office. I was not in power so it was not for me to examine the files. I did not know anything about Brennan and McGowan. I did not talk to Mr. Gogarty. I made some efforts with Bovale and JMSE. It was not a question that Members of this House did not know that money was received. During the 1997 election campaign I was asked by eminent journalists about Ray Burke and I made it absolutely clear that I was aware he had received money. That was written in several national newspapers. It was not illegal for him to receive that money. He said he had done nothing wrong. I took him at his word—

MR. [SEÁN] RYAN: It was an exceptionally large sum of money.

AN CEANN COMHAIRLE: Do not interrupt the Taoiseach, Deputy Ryan.

THE TAOISEACH: I took the man's word. I did not have the powers of a major five-year investigation. If I had all the information then that has taken five years to uncover, I would certainly not have appointed him.

MR. RABBITTE: Twenty five years of friendship.

'A SCANDALOUSLY RECKLESS, NEGLIGENT, PROFLIGATE DEAL'

Indemnity for religious congregations

Compensating victims of clerical sex abuse could cost Ireland more than a billion euro, the state's financial watchdog asserted in September 2003. Comptroller and Auditor General John Purcell, in his annual report, assessed the liability to the State at between €869 million and €1.04 billion. The Taoiseach Bertie Ahern claimed it would be nothing like it and that he was anticipating a 'far smaller' amount.

Mr. Ahern said the Government was committed to giving redress to victims and the indemnity deal struck with the religious congregations was a 'sensible way forward'. Labour leader Pat Rabbitte said that anyone describing it in those terms 'does not deserve to be in the Taoiseach's position' and that it was a disgrace for Mr. Ahern to dismiss Mr. Purcell's calculation. He claimed the Taoiseach had authorised former Education Minister Dr. Michael Woods to come to a 'secret' agreement with Church representatives. He described the €128 million indemnity for religious congregations as 'a scandalously reckless, negligent, profligate deal entered into in the name of the Irish taxpayer'.

(30 September 2003)

MR. [PAT] RABBITTE: I have raised with the Taoiseach many times in the House, including on four consecutive days last February, the question of the deal entered into with religious congregations. I made a number of points about the deficiency in the deal, but I made two points in particular. I said the Government grossly underestimated the liability and exposure of the taxpayer, which could amount to a total of €1 billion, and I pointed out that the Attorney General was not involved in the deed of indemnity

    After the Taoiseach denied my charges, defended the deal and misled the House as to the number of complainants, the Comptroller and Auditor General decided to undertake his own assessment, published today. In it he concludes that the total exposure of the State will be between €869 million and €1.04 billion and points out that, at the time, the Attorney General was excluded from involvement in the critical negotiations. Initially, the then Minister, Deputy Woods, had him excluded and refused even to reply to his letters. Later, at the critical time, he was campaigning in the general election, ironically seeking to prevent the Taoiseach from spending €1,000 million building on a football stadium at a time when a deal for €1,000 million was being concluded in his office when he was not present.

The report published today by a constitutional officer, the Comptroller and Auditor General, is the most serious indictment ever to come before the House of a scandalously reckless, negligent and profligate deal entered into in the name of Irish taxpayers by a Government, the facts surrounding which the Taoiseach attempted to cover up, deny, refute and then defend in this House. The findings of this report are far more serious than anything ever concluded on behalf of the State by the Taoiseach's mentor, the former Taoiseach, Charles Haughey, who has been the subject of much odium in the House. Any Government that concluded a deal like this does not deserve to be in the charge of the affairs of the country.

THE TAOISEACH [BERTIE AHERN]: I have previously said many things about this agreement. At the outset let me say I disagree with Deputy Rabbitte that I misled the House. It will take at least two years before an assessment of how many people will be included under the terms of the agreement can be known and the figures I have previously indicated continue to be the figures indicated by the various Departments and the Attorney General.

Deputy Rabbitte and I will never agree on the indemnity agreement but we can at least listen to each other's points of view. I will at all times listen to his. The Government was committed to giving redress by way of compensation to victims of abuse and we intend to do so. The redress board was established for this purpose. If we had not agreed to compensate victims of abuse through this mechanism, then each and every court case brought to the High Court—at that stage there were approximately 2,000 cases—would have had to be fought in the court. It would have been necessary to bring a claim for financial contribution in respect of each case against the religious orders, which would have taken years. The compensation payments would have been delayed in thousands of court sittings. There would also have been debates about limitation periods and the responsibility of religious orders for abusers, which would have been a nightmare scenario for the victims. Given that she could not get the legal people involved, Ms. Justice Laffoy was seeking to introduce a redress system and there was pressure on the Government to do so.

There is a commonly held belief, fostered by those who wish to confuse, that, somehow, the State was unwise to enter an indemnity agreement. I accept that Deputy Rabbitte continues to make that point.

MR. RABBITTE: I did not make that point and I never did so.

THE TAOISEACH: A number of facts demonstrate that this argument is without foundation. Indeed, in the view of this and the previous Government, concluding an agreement with the religious orders was in the best interest of the State. I remind the House that when the issue of responsibility between the state and the institutions was raised in the Canadian courts, according to a court decision the allocation of blame was 70% to the state and 30% to the religious orders. It is important in showing that the State had a major responsibility for what went on in these institutions. As I have said continuously, and it is why I apologised, we abandoned the children of another generation in these institutions and failed miserably to ensure their interests were protected.

MR. RABBITTE: We know that.

THE TAOISEACH: It seems that everyone agrees with that proposition, as Deputy Rabbitte has said. However, the logical conclusion that arises from this is that the State had to bear a significant proportion of the responsibility towards victims, and that is our view. In entering into the indemnity agreement, the State was conscious of the fact that victims could lose cases brought against religious orders, which would have been an appalling scenario. To arrange for the religious orders to make payments to the State, totalling €127 million, was in our view a sensible way to proceed.

As I have done so before, I can set out the reasons we believe many of these people would lose their cases. There are several problems in this area, one of which I wish to highlight. Under our law, where a victim obtains a judgment under civil liability legislation for a monetary sum, the total amount of the judgment would have to be paid by the State. It is a fundamental principle of our code that those who committed wrongs are liable for all of the injury or loss, even though they bear different degrees of responsibility. This means that even if one is only 1% responsible in law—the State's responsibility was certainly far higher than that—all of the damages must be paid, with recovery to be sought from other wrongdoers. The State would have ended up paying the money in any event.

I do not know what will be the final figure. Our view continues to be that it will not be anything like what the eminent Comptroller and Auditor General has said. We still believe it will be far smaller. However, we continue to faithfully hold the view that we would not have been able to deal with this issue if we did not establish a redress board and if we did not properly agree a compensation indemnity claim. We could have ended up with the worst of all scenarios, where the individuals would have received no money. That was our legal opinion then and now, and it remains the Government's view.

MR. RABBITTE:

It is disgraceful for the Taoiseach and his office to dismiss in this House the findings of the Comptroller and Auditor General as if it were an unfounded charge. Why did the Department of Finance recommend a 50-50 arrangement and why did the Government initially pursue that strategy if the Taoiseach considers it to be an unfair apportionment? Any Taoiseach who would say that a contribution of €127 million by the religious orders is a sensible way forward in a deal that the Comptroller and Auditor General estimates could cost of the order of €1 billion does not deserve to be in the Taoiseach's position.

How could he have entered into such a deal in circumstances where, according I understand to page 85 of the Comptroller and Auditor General's report, the Department of Education and Science said it was not legally competent to permit its Minister to sign the indemnity without the involvement of the Attorney General, while yet proceeding to sign off on it?

When the deal went to the Cabinet on the last day of the previous Government's term of office, the Department knew it was inadequate. On 29 June 2001, the Minister for Finance, Deputy McCreevy, had written to say he was disappointed with the contribution from the religious congregations based on the then assessment of €200 million to €400 million. If it was disappointing in that context, it is certainly disappointing in the context of €800 million to €1,000 million.

There is no explanation for this. The Attorney General was not at his desk. When he was, he was excluded by a decision by the then Minister for Education and Science, Deputy Woods, who attended the two critical meetings at which the deal was entered into. The then Minister has never told us why that happened. All the Taoiseach's Cabinet colleagues were involved, including the Tánaiste and Minister for Enterprise, Trade and Employment.

Who would have thought we have come to the stage where the Minister for Justice, Equality and Law Reform will not even come into the House? He was up lampposts when this major deal was being concluded and was nowhere in sight. On the last day he said it was a deficient deal and that it contained no mechanism to deal with the rising number of complainants, yet the Taoiseach signed off on it anyway. The Taoiseach sent out 'Woodsie' to agree a secret indemnity that was never debated in this House, he signed off on it and hoped it would never come back to haunt him, but it has done so.

Dr. [Michael] Woods:

For the record, there was debate in this House on numerous occasions.

An Ceann Comhairle [Rory O'Hanlon]:

Deputy Woods must find another way of making his point. I ask him to resume his seat. As it is Leaders' Questions, only party leaders may intervene.

The Taoiseach:

Whatever about the accusations Deputy Rabbitte makes about people being out campaigning, what he has stated is not true either. This matter was discussed repeatedly in the House and was long in the public domain.

Mr. Rabbitte:

The indemnity deal was never discussed.

An Ceann Comhairle:

Deputy Rabbitte should allow the Taoiseach to speak without interruption.

The Taoiseach:

The Government agreed in principle to establish a compensation scheme on 3 October 2000. There were meetings with the congregations on 10 November at which they indicated their intention to make a meaningful contribution. Further meetings were held on 27 November 2000, 2 and 21 February, 6 and 23 March, 4 and 30 April, 10 May, and 5 and 26 June. All meetings were attended by officials of the Department of Education and Science, the Department of Finance, the Office of the Attorney General and representatives of the congregations.

MR. RABBITTE: They went nowhere.

THE TAOISEACH: As discussions proceeded, the then Minister for Education and Science became involved resulting in a deal being agreed.

There is no comparable situation for these issues of which the Government is aware. The Canadian arrangement has worked. The State must bear a significant liability given that, in many cases of abuse, children had been taken from their homes by the State and placed in the care of religious orders, some of whose members abused them. In many cases State agencies were aware that institutions were being run under abusive regimes. Some institutions covered by the redress scheme were run by the State. There was 100% liability in many cases.

MR. RABBITTE: There was 100% liability?

THE TAOISEACH:	In many cases the State turned its back on its responsibility to cherish the children of the nation. If we were to adopt an alternative approach that would force victims to face—
MR. RABBITTE:	That is not the issue.
THE TAOISEACH:	It is.
AN CEANN COMHAIRLE:	Allow the Taoiseach to speak without interruption. His time has concluded.
THE TAOISEACH:	If we were to follow through Deputy Rabbitte's point, something on which he continually misleads the people—
MR. [SEÁN] RYAN:	The Taoiseach is trying to mislead to remove himself from this situation.
THE TAOISEACH:	—victims would face traumatic cross-examination by lawyers. It would take many years for the courts to finish hearing 2,000 to 4,000 cases. Many could be thrown out by the courts because of the amount of time that had elapsed since the abuse occurred. Much of the property of the congregations is tied up in trusts and would not be taken, even by the courts. The legal fees would be enormous. Some of the congregations which have contributed have few or

no claims against them.

The suggestion that the congregations have a great deal of money which can be taken is not true. The idea that schools, homes and institutions can be taken to be sold to put money in the redress fund is not true. Deputy Rabbitte continues to mislead people on this and he is wrong.

'WHEN YOU'RE GOING THROUGH HELL, KEEP GOING . . .'

Cullen admits his mistake on e-voting

'I accept I have taken a political hit,' the then Environment Minister Martin Cullen told the Dáil in May 2004. The Government's electronic voting dream was in tatters. The Independent Commission on Electronic Voting had given it the thumbs down, saying the security of the €50 million system could not be guaranteed in time for the following month's local and European elections. Labour's Eamon Gilmore claimed that the Government had made a decision to use electronic voting before it had legal authority to do so.

The Commission's findings were deeply embarrassing for the Government and for the Minister in particular who, for months, had been facing down all objections to the scheme's reliability from Opposition and other independent sources. A chastened Mr. Cullen admitted, 'With hindsight, I could have done much differently.' But he claimed he was drawing strength from the example of none other than Winston Churchill.

(06 May 2004)

MR. [MARTIN] CULLEN:	As I said in response to another Deputy I much prefer to do as Churchill said, when one is going through hell, keep going. I assure the Deputy I intend to come out the other side of it. He will not get me to lie down under—
MR. [BERNARD] ALLEN:	At least the Minister admits he is going through hell.
MR. [ARTHUR] MORGAN:	The Minister should not follow Churchill. He should not listen to Churchill.
MR. CULLEN:	I think it is a very good quote. It is one that has imbued me in the last few days and steeled me to keep going on this issue. The more I read the report, the more confident I am that what will come out of all of this will without question be—
MR. ALLEN:	The Minister is in serious denial.
MR. CULLEN:	I accept the Deputy is making a political point and I accept I have taken a political hit.
MR. ALLEN:	We are politicians and we will make political points.
MR. CULLEN:	I am big enough and long enough in this House to know that. The

other thing I know and I believe the Deputies opposite also know, is that electronic voting will be introduced in Ireland. Most of the western world has introduced electronic voting and even in the developing world, such as in India, it is being introduced. Ireland will also do so. Unfortunately, unlike the public in this country, who took to electronic voting with great gusto and gave it a substantial thumbs-up when the research was conducted following its use in the general election and in the referenda, the same cannot be said of the politicians opposite, even though the former Taoiseach and leader of Fine Gael went out with a brochure saying it was as simple as one, two, three. Obviously the current leader of Fine Gael—

MR. ALLEN:

On a point of order. The Minister is referring to a former Taoiseach. I read a letter into the record of the House yesterday which stated the views of the former Taoiseach. The Minister was shaking hands in Wexford yesterday. The former Taoiseach stated his views in correspondence with the present Taoiseach in April 2002.

AN LEAS-CHEANN COMHAIRLE [SÉAMUS PATTISON]:

The Deputy no longer has the floor because that is not a point of order.

MR. ALLEN:

The Minister should not make misleading statements.

AN LEAS-CHEANN COMHAIRLE:

The Deputy should not mislead the Chair.

MR. CULLEN:

To conclude on the point, I am happy to confirm to the House that the money invested in the technology and the electronic voting machines is secure. The machines will be secured. The Government will work with the commission. It will deal with any questions and recommendations from the commission and allay any concerns it may have. The Government will assist the commission with any testing if required. The commission is entitled to carry out the testing to satisfy itself. I look forward to the commission completing the testing it requires to be carried out. The commission's emphasis is clearly on the count software and not on the electronic voting machines. The report hardly refers to the electronic voting machines. The pages of the report referred to by Deputy Allen deal largely with the counting software which is separate.

MR. ALLEN: Are they not an important element in the whole set-up?

AN LEAS-CHEANN COMHAIRLE: Order, please.

MR. CULLEN: The commission is at pains to state it is not in a position to confirm one way or the other. It is interesting that the commission has stated that the burden of proof for giving a negative finding in its report is far lower than it would have been for a positive conclusion. I hope the commission will be in a position as soon as possible to have all the testing completed so we can move on from what is really a spurious debate. I look forward to seeing the system being vindicated. I am opposing the amendment.

MR. [EAMON] GILMORE: I will reply to the debate. I wish to refer in particular to a number of points made by the Minister. I agree with him on something; I agree the day will come when electronic voting will be used in Ireland. Contrary to the impression the Minister wishes to give, this debate was never about whether electronic voting would be used or not used. This debate was about the way in which it was being introduced and the system the Government wanted to introduce unilaterally, about which serious concerns had been raised.

I said yesterday and I repeat it today, as far as the Labour Party is concerned, there are two preconditions for the introduction of electronic voting.

MR. CULLEN:

Will the Deputy accept that no political party had any involvement in the procurement of the system?

MR. GILMORE:

I do not know that. Since the Minister has raised the question of the procurement of the system, there is an issue relating to the procurement of the system for which I have never received a satisfactory explanation. During the course of the Committee Stage debate, the Opposition was told that the tender for the system was advertised some time in the second half of 2000. That was my understanding of it. The tender competition took place sometime in the summer or autumn of 2000. I found it puzzling that the initial legislation allowing for electronic voting in the first place was not even published until Christmas 2000. I cannot recall if the Minister or the Minister of State was present during Committee Stage on that occasion. I referred to it on Committee Stage and I am puzzled how the Government could proceed to have a tender competition for a system when the enabling legislation had not been passed and no decision had been made. The Oireachtas had not decided to move to electronic voting and no law provided for it, yet the Government unilaterally decided to plough ahead with the competition and effectively committed the State and taxpayers to considerable sums of money before legislation was passed. We were told in the course of the debate in committee that the decision to proceed with the purchase, through tender, was based on a Government decision, which I understand was a formal one. This decision was not publicly announced at the time, nor was the House informed of it. Some information about it emerged during the Committee Stage debate of the Electoral (Amendment) Act 2001, with further information emerging later.

The Minister asked me to accept that no political party was involved in the procurement process. While I am not making such an accusation, in the circumstances I have described I am certainly not prepared at this point to accept that no party was involved in the procurement because the parties in Government were obviously party to a decision to buy a system before authority was given for it. That aspect of this matter, which I appreciate, arose before the Minister's appointment—

MR. CULLEN: If it is of benefit to the Deputy, I have been handed a note detailing the sequence.

MR. GILMORE: It may be useful to place it on the record, with the permission of the Chair.

MR. CULLEN: To avoid confusion as regards the point raised by Deputy Gilmore, I will outline the sequence. The Electoral (Amendment) Act 2001, which made legal provisions for the acquisition and use of electronic voting machinery, was enacted on 24 October 2001. The letter of intent, subject to conditions, to purchase 600 voting machines for the 2002 pilot at the general election issued on 16 November 2001. The Government, on 19 February 2002 subject to satisfactory testing of the system software approved the use of the system in the 2002 general election. The cost of the equipment used was not paid until after that date and well after the legislation was enacted. Expenditure on the purchase of six voting machines and testing costs in 2001 were paid out of the Department's Vote which was approved by the Dáil and by the Appropriation Act of that year. The tender submitted by Nedap-Powervote was accepted in January 2001 for phase one of the project, namely, the purchase of six voting machines and ancillary equipment.

MR. GILMORE:

That does not clarify the point I have been making. I am aware of the sequence beginning with the letter of intent which issued on 16 November 2001. My point is that the tender competition was held in 2000 before the legislation was published and either the Government, the Department, the Minister or his predecessor decided to accept the tender from Nedap-Powervote some time in late 2000 before the legislation was published.

The first question that arises, and one I posed in committee, is how was it decided to hold the tendering competition and then select the successful tender, in this case the Nedap-Powervote formula. That decision amounted essentially to selecting the system before the enabling legislation was even published. The answer to that question, when I raised it on committee, was that the decision to hold the tender competition and, as a consequence, select the successful Nedap-Powervote tender, was taken on foot of a Government decision.

In answer to the Minister's question as to whether I accept that no political party had an involvement in the selection of the Nedap-Powervote system, I cannot accept that statement because, according to what we were told on committee, the two Government parties made a decision, in Government and before the legislation was published or legal authority had been given to move to electronic voting, to hold a tender competition to select an electronic voting system. Moreover, the Nedap-Powervote system we are now debating was selected some time in late 2000 before the initial legislation was published. That was, therefore, a political decision, for which there was no legal authority or legislative basis. The House had not been consulted or informed.

MR. CULLEN: The Deputy is correct in stating a Government policy decision was taken. Governments make policy decisions all the time.

MR. GILMORE: No Government can commit—

MR. CULLEN: The Government was not involved in the procurement process.

MR. GILMORE: The Minister is shifting the question. The Government is not omnipotent and while it may not appreciate it, it is accountable to the House.

MR. CULLEN: I accept that.

MR. GILMORE: The Government made a decision to use electronic voting and select a system before it had legal authority to do so. I do not know what was the motivation for this decision or what was pushing it because the House has not been told, but I will not give a blanket absolution to the political parties in Government that they had nothing to do with selecting the system. They had everything to do with it because they took the decision.

The Minister is clutching at one page of the report of the Commission on Electronic Voting, namely, page 19, for comfort in these, his hours of trauma about the electronic voting system, but ignores what the commission stated about the system. Basically, the report states that while the software being used has been updated many times, the Minister continues to rely on tests or reviews done on earlier desk versions of the software. It states that some components of the system have not been tested, the source code is not available and the tests carried out to date are insufficient to establish its reliability for use at elections in June. It also points out that end to end testing had not been carried out in full or independently.

MR. CULLEN: I do not have an issue with the report. If that is the view of the commission, that is fine. If it wants to carry out testing to replicate testing already carried out, that is fine with me. I do not have an argument with the commission.

MR. ALLEN: The Minister is incredible and irresponsible.

MR. CULLEN: What does the Deputy propose I do? The commission has given its subjective view. One group told me the system is efficient, while another group takes a different view. That leaves me in the middle.

MR. ALLEN: He is behaving like an ostrich.

ACTING CHAIRMAN [DINNY McGINLEY]: Allow Deputy Gilmore to continue without interruption, please.

MR. GILMORE: If the Minister had made that statement last autumn, we would not have wasted months debating the issue.

MR. CULLEN: With hindsight, I could have done much differently, particularly if I had been responsible from the outset.

MR. ALLEN: He should have listened occasionally.

MR. GILMORE: Hindsight is great. As someone once told me, the cruellest thing one can say to anybody is 'I told you so', but I will not labour the point.

The point is that the commission has found that this was not properly tested and that it needs to be fully tested. I have only one difficulty with the assurances the Minister is now giving. We tabled two amendments yesterday and the Government defeated them. One amendment stated that this should be done by all-party agreement, but the Government voted against it. This seems to indicate that there is still an intention to run with this issue unilaterally. I proposed the other amendment, which stated that we should not proceed with electronic voting until the commission gives it the green light. The Government again voted against the amendment.

This is a flawed Bill as the commission is confined to looking at the Nedap-Powervote system. The Minister may choose other systems if he wants to do so. There is no legal requirement that the system can only proceed with the agreement of the commission or on the basis of a sufficient level of political consensus. For all these reasons, this is a flawed Bill.

I am prepared to accept the Minister's statement that the Attorney General's office and the parliamentary counsel are satisfied with the technical and legal issues which arise in the amendment and I will withdraw it.

MR. CULLEN: I would have had no wish to be here all week if I did not think the Bill was necessary. The basic problem that forced me to come in here was that I had to give the commission a statutory basis. I am not here for any other reason. There are other issues which I am legally obliged to get in situ before the election. As a politician, the Deputy knows that we would be much better off if this was not happening this week and that the issue had passed on the basis of the report. I agree with him and have fundamental views on the operation and running of elections in this country. These views are not far from what he has been saying in the House.

However, there is a commission sitting that has been charged by all of us to report and it should be allowed to do that job. It may do the State a great service if there is something fundamentally wrong of which I am unaware. This will only happen if it is allowed time and the right to carry out specific testing. I am persuaded by august international institutes which have examined the system and informed me that it is perfect. I am not a technical expert but I cannot ignore that kind of advice. With hindsight there may have been a number of problems, but one finds oneself with what one has and tries to plot a way through it.

I also agree that there should be an objective of all-party agreement. If I made one mistake, it was a presumption, after the pilot phases and the public reviews, that there was one clear issue which arose, namely, the presentation of the results. I immediately tried to resolve this in the committee and acknowledged the issue in parliamentary questions in the Dáil to much acclaim. I stated that I would change how the results were presented and go back to the old way of doing it count by count. That was the major issue at the time, not the current issue. I thought we still had a general consensus on this issue. That was my position, but it was a mistake or, rather, a presumption. I should have tested it with the House at that time. That is hindsight and I wish I could reverse the clock to think it through.

It was a reasonable presumption at the time. I had no grounds, on contractual commitments, to sunder the system when the decision was made in December 2000 to roll it out fully after the pilot stages. I could not expose the State to massive lawsuits. The Deputy has accepted my point on the amendment, but I agree that there are issues.

'LEAKS AND CRACKS'

The National Aquatic Centre

In June 2005, reports emerged that water was leaking from cracks in the National Aquatic Centre. Responding to Opposition jibes, the Taoiseach Bertie Ahern claimed he was proud to claim the facility as a 'pet project'. Fine Gael leader Enda Kenny demanded that he explain who was responsible for the fact that the roof had blown off the building. 'The wind,' the Taoiseach shot back. He continued to insist the centre was fully operational.

'It is leaking,' Labour's Liz McManus reminded him.

(28 June 2005)

MR. [ENDA] KENNY: Very few people in the country will forget the description, in May 2002, of the campus Ireland project by the Minister for Justice, Equality and Law Reform as being 'Ceaucescu-like', but recent revelations suggest that this analogy might not be as far-fetched as people imagined. After all, the infamous Romanian tyrant left behind him a battery of extravagant, egotistical, sub-standard, unfinished monuments and buildings, the price for which his people will continue to pay for many years to come. The debacle of the National Aquatic Centre truly is an apt metaphor for the Fianna Fáil-Progressive Democrats Government—massive costs to the public, a so-called state-of-the-art attraction that is all splash, with fake waves, the roof blown off and leaking like a sieve.

I put it to the Taoiseach that, as the sole promoter and shareholder of this project, he is personally responsible for the huge failures that have been exposed. Does the Taoiseach stand over his statement at the opening of the centre on 10 March 2003 that 'a visionary concept has been brought to magnificent fruition'? Will the Taoiseach confirm that the facility is leaking water at the rate of 5 million litres per month and that a consultant's report has found that the original roof structure was substandard, suggesting that either corners were cut or plans were washed away at the construction stage? Were these facts known to the Minister for Arts, Sport and Tourism, who claimed two weeks ago that the €62 million capital expenditure on the project 'represents money very well spent' or can we take it that this farce is the benchmark, or rather the tide mark, of Government spending and standards?

THE TAOISEACH [BERTIE AHERN]:

Campus and Stadium Ireland Development has stated that the reports in the media relating to the National Aquatic Centre are inaccurate in most respects and it would be inappropriate to comment on any of these issues as there are proceedings before the court.

MR. [BERNARD] DURKAN:

It might also be embarrassing to have to comment on the issues.

(Interruptions.)

THE TAOISEACH:

The proceedings are before the court. Yesterday, CSID's legal team referred to the situation which has grown murkier and murkier—

MR. DURKAN:

Curiouser and curiouser.

THE TAOISEACH:

I advise all concerned to allow the courts—

(Interruptions.)

THE TAOISEACH:

Everyone should allow the courts to deal with the issue and not be fooled by red herrings, because that is what yesterday's furore in the media is about. I am very sad to see the Opposition aligning itself with the company that CSID has taken to court and acting as its mouthpiece in the House today. Opposition Deputies appear to have no compunction about making public statements on matters before the courts.

I agree with CSID that court proceedings should not be prejudiced and will not attempt to prejudge the outcome of the court's deliberations. Once the court proceedings have been completed, CSID will no longer be constrained from putting the facts before the public and any questions Deputies, the media or anyone else may have about the various matters before the court.

(Interruptions.)

THE TAOISEACH: I am happy to outline the factual position for the House. CSID has a legal action in the commercial court against Dublin Waterworld, the operator of the aquatic centre, for breaches of the lease agreement. In the commercial court on 3 June Mr. Justice Peter Kelly made an order regarding the following matters which were the subject of a statement of claim lodged by CSID against Dublin Waterworld.

(Interruptions.)

THE TAOISEACH: The dispute as to whether Dublin Waterworld is liable to pay VAT of €10,254,600 on the granting of the lease has been referred to arbitration which will be concluded shortly. The dispute regarding repair and maintenance and as to whether Dublin Waterworld has properly maintained the national aquatic centre has been referred to an architect for expert determination. This process is under way as per the court ruling.

On the question of the lease, the remaining issues against Dublin Waterworld for failure to pay rent, the failure to provide audited accounts, thus preventing the profit share to be circulated; the failure to pay insurance on the building; and the failure to establish a sinking fund, are still subject to court proceedings—

(Interruptions.)

AN CEANN COMHAIRLE: Please allow the Taoiseach to continue without interruption.

MR. DURKAN:	Literally, it has already sunk.
THE TAOISEACH:	I am reading from the court order.
MR. [RICHARD] BRUTON:	The court jester.
THE TAOISEACH:	If Opposition members want to make fun of Mr. Justice Kelly's order, that is a matter for them.
	Deputy Burton has been claiming that the national aquatic centre is a pet project of mine. I wish to confirm to the House that this is the case. I am proud to claim it as such. The motivation of the Government in developing the centre in the first place was to provide a 50 metre pool for the country and, specifically, a suitable location for hosting the aquatic events of the Special Olympics. The project was delivered on time and within budget.
MR. DURKAN:	As were the cracks in the concrete.
AN CEANN COMHAIRLE:	The Taoiseach's time is up.
THE TAOISEACH:	I only need another minute; I have injury time. Opposition members are giddy because they are getting their holidays.

(Interruptions.)

AN CEANN
COMHAIRLE:

Please allow the Taoiseach to continue without interruption.

MR. [PAUL] KEHOE:

He will be on his holidays.

THE TAOISEACH:

The national aquatic centre has drawn well deserved admiration from those who have visited and used the facilities since the centre was opened just over two years ago.

MS. [LIZ] MCMANUS:

It is leaking.

THE TAOISEACH:

It has successfully hosted the Special Olympics Summer Games and later in the same year the European short course championships, both to significant acclaim. In its first year of operation it had close to 1 million visitors which placed it among the top attractions in the country.

(Interruptions.)

THE TAOISEACH:

It continues to be equally popular as a facility for those who love water sports, especially young people, tourists and swimmers of all ages and abilities. Deputy Kenny has referred to a statement made last week by my colleague, the Minister for Arts, Sport and Tourism, who said the capital expenditure provision represented value for money. I fully agree with him.

MS. [OLIVIA] MITCHELL:

It is time to retire.

MR. KENNY:

I am glad to receive confirmation from the Taoiseach that this is his pet project and that, therefore, he knows all about it.

THE TAOISEACH:

It is one of them.

MR. KENNY:

Will the Taoiseach explain who is responsible for the fact that the roof blew off the building—

THE TAOISEACH:

The wind.

(Interruptions.)

AN CEANN COMHAIRLE:

Please allow Deputy Kenny to continue without interruption.

MR. KEHOE:

I hope they can put it back up in the Taoiseach's constituency office in St. Luke's.

THE TAOISEACH:

While I am hugely powerful, I am not the one who will organise it.

MR. KENNY:	I remind the Taoiseach that the wind also blew over a lot of other rooftops, none of which blew off.
THE TAOISEACH:	It blew off a lot of them.
MR. KENNY:	Who is responsible for the inferior construction of the building and the fact that 5 million litres of treated water is leaking out on a monthly basis?

(Interruptions.)

MR. KENNY:	Does the Taoiseach stand over the remarks he made about the shelf company on 26 March 2002, that despite being a shelf company, it was a company not only of substance but of international standing? It was criticised in the High Court yesterday when Mr. Justice Kelly queried the reason a company worth €127 should be given a 30 year lease on an asset worth €62 million. Does the Taoiseach now stand over that statement? Has the company lived up to his expectations? Will he stand over the arrangements whereby the Government entered into an agreement with the company which was sharply criticised in the High Court?

I was in the Mansion House last

night to welcome the new Lord Mayor of Dublin, Councillor Catherine Byrne. In the middle of all the pomp and power, I noticed the coat of arms of the Ahern family whose motto reads—

MS. [KATHLEEN] LYNCH:

Water wings.

MR. KENNY:

—Per ardua surgo, I rise through difficulties. As the Taoiseach is nearing his escape from the House for his summer holidays, how does he intend to deal with this matter? Does he plan to wade, swim or dive through the difficulties?

MR. DURKAN:

I suggest he change the motto.

THE TAOISEACH:

Since Deputy Kenny has asked for my opinion, the Government is not happy with the performance of the company. While it has done a very good job in Killarney in the Kerry operation, it has not done a good job in this case. That is the reason CSID has brought the company to court. I support the action being taken. Obviously, I do not stand over the remarks made at the time.

I have already answered the question of what happened on 1

January. People have been critical of the damage caused by the freak storm. It is unfortunate it damaged a large number of buildings in the area, uprooted 200 year old trees and hit the centre. A report on the damage was commissioned by the OPW following a request from the Department of Arts, Sport and Tourism in consultation with CSID. Its findings were taken into account in agreeing the repair programme with the contractor. Legal, contractual and financial issues are being considered in the light of the report.

Our primary concern at all times must be to protect the taxpayer's investment and that is what we are doing. In spite of all the exaggerations in the newspapers about leaks and cracks, the national aquatic centre is fully operational—

MR. DURKAN: In the Government.

THE TAOISEACH: —and bringing endless enjoyment to adults and children, day in, day out, as well as providing a top class facility for our swimming athletes. I was in it ten days ago for a national swimming competition in which children and teenagers from all over the country participated. Because the issues are being dealt with in the courts, CSID are constrained from dealing with them in the media while it is fighting in the courts. I want to see the company win the case and compel Dublin Waterworld to pay. I hope the necessary legal process will resolve the issue.

PART Five

Coalition Tensions

'THIS PARTICULARLY RICKETY COALITION'

The 'unhappy history of the Progressive Democrats and Fianna Fáil'

On the opening day in the Dáil for the first Ahern administration in June 1997, Pat Rabbitte (then Democratic Left) congratulated each Minister in the Cabinet, 'even if they are members of a fairly rickety coalition'. Echoing former Taoiseach Albert Reynold's famous description of a 'temporary little arrangement' with the PDs, Mr. Rabbitte's assessment of the current partnership was that it was 'a very tentative arrangement indeed'.

He claimed that without Michael McDowell, 'one of the most able Deputies ever elected to this House' (who had lost his seat in the '97 election) the PDs were missing their 'ideological drive and cutting edge'. He warned the Progressive Democrats they would have less influence on Government policy than Kilgarvin, home to Fianna Fáil-friendly Independent Jackie Healy-Rae.

Indeed Deputy Rabbitte was now predicting tremendous improvements in Kerry South, having 'listened in amazement earlier as Deputy Healy-Rae listed the defects and handicaps under which people in that constituency have laboured for so long'. Deputy Healy-Rae had been pledging support for the new Taoiseach 'on the clear understanding that the problems in Kerry South will be addressed'.

Mr. Rabbitte had earlier teased Mr. Ahern about his choice of Minister for Health 'somebody with the sensitive touch of Deputy Cowen' who now also had responsibility for children.

He also noted that his own replacement as so-called 'Super Junior' Minister, PD Bobby Molloy, had previously railed against the creation of the position he now held—that of Minister of State entitled to attend Cabinet but not to vote.

(26 June 1997)

MR. [PAT] RABBITTE: I congratulate my constituency colleague, Deputy Harney. On a personal basis and on behalf of my constituents, I am very pleased at her elevation to a very significant economic ministry.

Of course, I am also delighted for Deputy Molloy who ranted and railed until the cows came home about the very post he now holds when it was established some three years ago.

(Interruptions.)

MRS. [NORA] OWEN: Superman.

MR. RABBITTE: I am not suggesting that Deputy Molloy can adequately fill the seat he now occupies but I will give him my full support in endeavouring to do the best he can with it.

No incoming Government in the history of this State has inherited from its immediate predecessor a country or economy in the condition of that being handed over today. There has been and continues to be unprecedented economic growth and historically low interest rates that have attracted investment and led to very low mortgage repayments. Forced emigration is a thing of the past. Annually an additional 50,000 of our people are at work and paying tax. That is a legacy no other Government has inherited. Notwithstanding the propitious economic circumstances about which I have spoken, I do not know whether this particularly rickety coalition Government will, as the Tánaiste, Deputy Harney, prophesied, lead this country into the new millennium. I do not believe it will.

The two parties that set out as an alliance of convenience—there was no other alliance available prior to the general election—an alliance between the largest party in the State and a party of a very different political character, have ended up as an alliance of grossly unequals. It seems the Progressive Democrat Party is the wren on the tail of the Fianna Fáil eagle, an eagle that is soaring high on a wind of transfers that were unreciprocated in the recent general election. For parties that lectured the people about how unstable would be an arrangement whereby the outgoing rainbow coalition Government was dependent on a gaggle of Independents, they have ended up in precisely that arrangement. Why would such an arrangement be unstable for the outgoing coalition Government but stable for this combination of parties? Considering the cohesive and stable reputation of the outgoing Government as distinct from the very unhappy history of the Progressive Democrats and Fianna Fáil, and their inability to coexist, this is a very tentative arrangement indeed.

I suggest that Kilgarvan and Kilcoole will have more influence in this Government than will the Progressive Democrats, and in the interests of the country one must ask whether that is healthy. I am very pleased the people of Kilcoole will get their second level school, and if I am sceptical about the Taoiseach's capacity to deliver longer summers in Kilgarvan and South Kerry, one can imagine the discomfiture of the Progressive Democrats. The ability of the Taoiseach to deliver longer evenings in Kerry is certainly not a recipe for stable, strong Government committed to fiscal rectitude, as promised by Fianna Fáil and the Progressive Democrats during the election campaign.

This is a most unlikely coalition comprising Fianna Fáil and a faction of Fianna Fáil that broke away in disgust and frustration with the party some years ago on fundamental issues of low standards in high places and playing politics with Northern Ireland. The new Tánaiste, Deputy Harney, assures us that all has changed, and perhaps it has, but what is the raison d'e tre of the Progressive Democrats? If there are no real policy distinctions with Fianna Fáil, why remain outside the fold? The departure of Michael McDowell, one of the most able Deputies ever elected to this House, has deprived the party of the ideological drive and cutting edge that was the Progressive Democrats. The ground is probably being assiduously prepared to monitor the reentry of the Progressive Democrats to Fianna Fáil and to join with those who would in other circumstances stand by the Republic.

There is no sign in the new Government's programme of fundamental Progressive Democrats policy positions. For example, none of the fundamental issues of difference enunciated during the election campaign, such as EMU privatisation, cuts in the public service and Northern Ireland, appears in the programme. Nor is there any trace of a commitment to implement the anti-poverty strategy devised by the former Minister of Social Welfare, Deputy Proinsias De Rossa. There are many omissions and several contradictions in the programme. As Deputy Bruton and Deputy Spring said, how is it possible to reconcile tax cuts for the best off in society with a rhetorical commitment to an inclusive society? It appears social equity will be abandoned in favour of pay back time for the better off. It is unfortunate the direction of the major programme of equitable integrated tax and social welfare system reform initiated by the outgoing Government is to be abandoned and replaced with a set of promises that will benefit only the better off. Nor is it possible to reconcile the new Administration's commitment to zero tolerance with its parallel pledge in respect of drug courts. The two policies are again opposites, one illiberal and the other liberal. One must ask which approach will win through? I suspect that neither will do so.

I am delighted that Deputy O'Donoghue has been appointed as Minister for Justice, Equality and Law Reform. It is not often that someone from, as Deputy Healy-Rae stated, a constituency as neglected as Kerry South obtains a senior Cabinet ministry. There must be other reasons that the Taoiseach recognised Deputy O'Donoghue's inherent qualities to appoint him to that position. However, the Deputy has left a terrible legacy in Kerry South. I listened in amazement earlier as Deputy Healy-Rae listed the defects and handicaps under which people in that constituency have laboured for so long. I have no doubt that, following Deputy Healy-Rae's election to the House, we will see tremendous improvements in Kerry South. I am happy about that and I propose to visit the area in the near future.

ACTING CHAIRMAN (SÉAMUS KIRK): The Deputy is beginning to exceed the time available to him.

MR. COWEN: The evenings are getting longer.

MR. RABBITTE: If I am, all I will do on this occasion is promise that it will be the first of many times I will attempt to do so.

'A LONG AND DARK SHADOW'

Des O'Malley denounces Haughey's legacy

In February 1999, PD founder Des O'Malley warned that his party could only continue in Government with Fianna Fáil while there was trust and confidence between the two Coalition partners. This was on the night Beverley Cooper-Flynn voted against the Government on the motion calling on her father, Padraig Flynn, to respond to allegations against him.

Mr. O'Malley said that Irish politics was still trying to emerge from the 'long and dark shadow' former Taoiseach Charlie Haughey had cast. Anticipating the rise of Sinn Féin, he warned Government deputies to stop acting the 'cute hoor' and deal decisively with sleaze and corruption.

(10 February 1999)

MR. [DES] O'MALLEY: With the benefit of hindsight, I can see more clearly than before why certain leading figures in Fianna Fáil, Mr. Flynn being notable among them, were so opposed to the notion of coalition with the Progressive

Democrats in 1989. Could it be they were afraid that we would cramp their style of doing business?

The next few months could be crucial in the political life of this country. We as a nation will be asked serious questions as to what kind of society, what kind of values and what kind of country we want. There may be further revelations made by tribunals, inquiries or the media, of wrongdoing at the highest levels in Irish society. If there are, they may be shocking and disturbing to most members of the voting public. For example, today's newspapers report a tribunal yesterday as having discovered that one of the providers of money—£100,000—to a Haughey family company was Mr. Michael Murphy, who has been a close associate of, and long time insurance broker, to Mr. Larry Goodman. He helped to negotiate Mr. Goodman's earliest export credit insurance cover for Iraq and he was also insurance broker to the Department of Agriculture and Food until it sued him last December in respect of huge losses it sustained in a major fire at a beef intervention store at Ballaghaderreen in 1992.

Politicians will have a clear choice in how they respond to any such revelations. They can choose to respond with courage, integrity and determination to eradicate the cancer of corruption that has poisoned the political and commercial affairs of this country in recent years or they may choose to shirk their responsibility. They may choose to act the 'cute hoor' yet again. They may choose to turn a blind eye, look the other way and indicate their tacit toleration and acceptance of a culture of crookedness and corruption. The people will then have a choice.

We may not have a general election for two or three years but events may dictate otherwise. Whenever the next election is held the question of standards in public life is likely to be one of the main items on the political agenda, if not the main item. What kind of standards do people want? What kind of parties do they want? What kind of politicians do they want? Will they believe those who say that all these tribunals are only barrister-fattening exercises, a waste of time and money and that we do not want to be digging into all that class of thing in any event? Would they vote for the brown envelope brigade if these gentlemen presented themselves for election again or are they prepared to make a genuine break with the past and embrace a new political order, one that gives precedence to decency over expediency, to honesty over dishonesty and to the public interest over the vested interest?

This Government has been surprisingly successful. It has made enormous progress in creating jobs, reducing unemployment and improving the lot of pensioners. The recent budget, for example, was a radical and reforming initiative by any standard. I take my hat off to Deputy Mary Harney for succeeding where others failed in introducing tax credits. It is a successful Government and we in the Progressive Democrats would like to see it continue in office.

However, it can continue in office only while there is trust and confidence between the two coalition partners. The position of the Progressive Democrats is straightforward. We do not expect people in public life to be saints or paragons of virtue. All we ask is that those in public life, especially those in high political office, abide by normal and reasonable standards of honesty and decency in dealing with the affairs of State.

If we are to be criticised for holding that position then this democracy is in more trouble than any of us realise. It is a well worn cliché that politics is on trial in this country, but that cliché has never been truer than it is now. The public is interested to see revealed what the politicians of the 1980s got up to. They are also interested to see how those revelations will be dealt with by the politicians of the 1990s. All of us in this House can help to restore public confidence in the Irish political system or we can abandon our responsibility. If we abandon our responsibility to deal decisively with sleaze and corruption we run the risk of abandoning democracy itself.

There is a political movement out there now, watching current developments very closely. That movement has recently put itself forward as the real anti-sleaze party in Irish politics. I refer to the so-called republican movement, the people who murdered Jerry McCabe. Increasingly, public cynicism about politics is creating political space which these people are glad to occupy. The last time I made a speech in this House about my vision of a republic I got into a lot of trouble about it. However, my idea of a republic is very different from that of those who murder gardaí and mutilate for life those with whom they disagree.

We have a chance to restore the public's faith in politics over the next few months and an opportunity to show that this Republic is run by decent people according to decent standards. Let us embrace that opportunity.

'THE MISSING BIT'

Hugh O'Flaherty's nomination to the European Investment Bank

In May 2000, the Cabinet nominated the former Supreme Court Judge Hugh O'Flaherty for the post of vice-president of the European Investment Bank [EIB].

This was described by Fine Gael's Michael Noonan as 'the greatest comeback since Lazarus'. Mr. O'Flaherty had resigned from the Supreme Court the previous year following the controversial release of Dublin architect Philip Sheedy after Sheedy served just one year of a four-year sentence (for drunk driving and dangerous driving causing death).

An inquiry by Chief Justice Liam Hamilton had described Mr. O'Flaherty's intervention in the case as motivated by humanitarian concerns, but 'open to misinterpretation.' In a radio interview on 20 June, the Taoiseach suggested it would be a good idea for Mr. O'Flaherty to give an account of his role in the matter, making cryptic remarks about a 'missing bit' in the Sheedy affair. Immediately, not only the Opposition but also the Tánaiste demanded clarification. However, the Taoiseach told the House the following morning that he was still fully behind Mr. O'Flaherty's nomination. That afternoon, while Finance Minister Charlie McCreevy fielded questions on the controversy, Independent Socialist Joe Higgins offered another spin on the story: the Taoiseach had 'responded in the usual way by speaking out of both sides of his mouth at once and allowed the hapless Tánaiste, Deputy Harney, to carry the can.'

Mr. O'Flaherty subsequently made the decision to withdraw his name for nomination.

(21 June 2000)

MR. [MICHAEL] NOONAN:	Was the Minister for Finance briefed by the Taoiseach or his officials prior to coming into the House to answer these questions? Was he briefed about the contents of the Taoiseach's radio interview? If he was briefed, will he explain to the House what was in the Taoiseach's mind? If he has not been briefed, will he explain to the House what he is doing here this afternoon?
MR. [CHARLIE] MCCREEVY:	I am here to answer questions because I am the Minister for Finance, the Minister responsible for processing the nomination of Mr. Hugh O'Flaherty to the European Investment Bank.
MR. NOONAN:	Was the Minister briefed by the Taoiseach or his officials on the subject

matter of all the questions, particularly of those questions transferred from the Taoiseach's office to the Minister to be answered here? The Ceann Comhairle has informed the House that any Minister may answer and that the Minister for Finance is the appropriate person to answer. Now it seems that the Minister is dodging the subject matter of the majority of questions which have been tabled.

MR. [DERMOT] AHERN:

The Deputy is answering his own question.

MR. NOONAN:

I will come to the Deputy later, unless he is up a tree somewhere investigating something.

MR. D. AHERN:

Anytime.

MR. MCCREEVY:

The Deputy's question asked if I have forwarded the name of Mr. Hugh O'Flaherty to the European Investment Bank, if I still intend proceeding with the appointment of Mr. O'Flaherty to the position as the vice president of the bank and if I will make a statement on the matter. I have answered that.

MR. [RÚAIRÍ] QUINN:

Does the Minister for Finance agree with the Taoiseach that Mr.

Hugh O'Flaherty should avail of an opportunity as soon as possible to explain what was referred to as the 'missing bit' in the whole sorry, sad Sheedy saga? Has the Taoiseach conveyed to the Minister for Finance his interpretation of what that missing bit might be? Is the missing bit contained in the comprehensive briefing notes the Minister is now reading?

MR. MCCREEVY: I understand that Mr. O'Flaherty is giving wide ranging interviews to news organisations as we speak and I am sure all relevant questions have been put to him.

MR. QUINN: Did the Minister for Finance discuss the content of his reply with the Taoiseach before answering this question?

MR. MCCREEVY: As Deputy Quinn is aware from his long experience as a member of Government, all members of the Cabinet share collective responsibility.

MR. QUINN: That is not what I asked. Has the Minister discussed the contents of his reply with the Taoiseach? The Minister is being remarkably arrogant.

Mr. Howlin: The Minister is supposed to be accountable. This is most unsatisfactory.

Mr. [Jim] Higgins: Was the Minister for Finance at the Cabinet meeting on Friday 16 April 1999 when a collective decision was made by him and other members of the Cabinet to write to Mr. O'Flaherty to inform him that the Government had decided to forward the report of the Chief Justice to the Oireachtas Committee on Justice, Equality and Women's Rights, and to advise him that the Government would consider at its meeting the following Tuesday proposing resolutions for the consideration of the two Houses of the Oireachtas, pursuant to Article 35.4.1° of the Constitution, for his removal on the grounds that the facts admitted to the Chief Justice, or established by him in his report, amounted to misbehaviour? Was the Minister at that Cabinet meeting? Why did he write to Mr. O'Flaherty in those terms? Why, if Mr. O'Flaherty was deemed unsuitable to remain as a Supreme Court judge, should he now be deemed suitable for a senior position as vice-president of the

European Investment Bank with a salary of £170,000?

MR. McCREEVY: Deputy Jim Higgins, as a former member of the Cabinet and spokesman on justice, equality and law reform, is aware there was a Supreme Court decision regarding Cabinet confidentiality and that it is not possible for members of the Cabinet to confirm or deny what has gone on in Cabinet.

MRS. [NORA] OWEN: Was the Minister there?

MR. [JOHN] BRUTON: Is the Minister aware that the Taoiseach said on the radio yesterday evening that Mr. O'Flaherty had questions to answer about his involvement in the Sheedy case?

MR. McCREEVY: As Deputy John Bruton is aware, because there is an outstanding picture of him standing in the office adjoining mine, Ministers for Finance have very little time to be listening to the radio.

MR. [BRENDAN] HOWLIN: That is appalling arrogance.

MRS. OWEN: A disgraceful answer.

MR. BRUTON: Will the Minister for Finance answer the question I asked. He has had notice of it. He should perhaps read the question in front of him. What are the questions which should be answered by Mr. O'Flaherty in the collective view of the Government and the Taoiseach? If Mr. O'Flaherty is prepared to answer those questions on a radio show, how can he justify his refusal to answer them before a committee of this House? Is the Minister happy with a situation in which a former judge will answer questions on a radio show but refuses point blank to answer them before a committee of this House?

Is the Government satisfied with that anomalous situation?

MR. McCREEVY: This is the third occasion on which I indicated to the House my reasons for putting forward the name of former Mr. Justice Hugh O'Flaherty as our nominee to the European Investment Bank. I am satisfied that Mr. O'Flaherty is the most outstanding candidate we could put forward at present.

MR. HOWLIN: The Minister should answer the questions he was asked.

MR. McCREEVY: I am not in a position to answer

any questions on behalf of Mr. O'Flaherty.

MR. BRUTON: Will the Minister—

AN LEAS-CHEANN COMHAIRLE [RORY O'HANLON]: I apologise, Deputy Bruton, but I must call Deputy Joe Higgins. Each of the previous speakers has had an opportunity to ask two supplementary questions; therefore, I must call on Deputy Higgins at this point.

MR. BRUTON: The Minister did not answer my question.

AN LEAS-CHEANN COMHAIRLE: I will call on Deputy Bruton again later.

MR. [JOE] HIGGINS: Does the Minister for Finance agree that this sorry saga highlights the fact that the traditional practice exercised by Fianna Fáil and other major parties in Government of nominating favoured people and cronies to important positions to which their qualifications are not relevant has been completely discredited? Does he also agree that the Taoiseach's remarks on radio last evening in relation to Mr. O'Flaherty's appointment represent nothing more than a cynical attempt to distance Fianna Fáil from a decision which opinion polls have shown was rejected outright by a large majority of ordinary people? Instead of defending a Cabinet decision, the Taoiseach, when confronted with a crisis, responded in the usual way by speaking out of both sides of his mouth at once and allowed the hapless Tánaiste, Deputy Harney, to carry the can.

AN LEAS-CHEANN COMHAIRLE:

A question please, Deputy.

MR. J. HIGGINS:

Does not this entire saga show that the Government is in almost complete disarray and that the situation cannot be remedied by any action the Minister for Finance might propose to take? Did the Minister discuss the situation which has developed in the past 24 hours with the Tánaiste? Will it be necessary to hold another bonding session in a villa in the south of France to repair the damage that has been done or have we passed that stage? Will we be faced with a general election in the near future as a result of the fallout from this affair?

MR. MCCREEVY:

On the Order of Business this morning the Taoiseach stated that, 'The Government is collectively responsible for the nomination of Mr.

Hugh O'Flaherty to the European Investment Bank. As leader of the Government I fully stand over that decision. With all my colleagues we made the decision. The Government had no reason to believe anything untoward needed to be added by way of explanation with regard to the controversy surrounding the Sheedy affair.'

MR. BRUTON:

I have no intention of annoying the Minister but I believe that the questions which were—

AN LEAS-CHEANN COMHAIRLE:

I wish to make clear to Members that from this point on questions will be taken on the basis of the proportionality of the parties. I will call the leaders of parties first.

MR. BRUTON:

Will the Minister indicate what the Taoiseach meant when he said that Mr. O'Flaherty has questions to answer about the 'missing bit'?

MR. McCREEVY:

I understand that, during the course of his radio interview, the Taoiseach stated that it is always open for Justice Hugh O'Flaherty to 'give his account of it'. I also understand that Mr. O'Flaherty has availed of that opportunity by giving a number of radio and television interviews.

MR. BRUTON: Given that the Minister nominated Mr. O'Flaherty to become a member of the EIB and in light of the fact that Mr. O'Flaherty has given interviews on radio, what does the Minister think of Mr. O'Flaherty's point blank refusal to answer questions before a committee of the House which represents the people of Ireland?

MR. MCCREEVY: I understand Mr. O'Flaherty outlined his position on that matter on the relevant occasion in 1999.

MR. BRUTON: Does the Minister not agree that there is a complete contradiction between Mr. O'Flaherty's willingness to answer questions on a talk show and his refusal to answer the same questions before the elected Assembly of the Irish people? Does he agree that Mr. O'Flaherty's behaviour is completely contrary to any understanding of democratic accountability?

MR. MCCREEVY: I made the decision to nominate Hugh O'Flaherty as the Government's candidate for membership of the board of the European Investment Bank and I took into account his qualifications and qualities when making that decision. I am quite satisfied that Mr. O'Flaherty is the most outstanding candidate Ireland has ever put forward for that position.

MR. QUINN:

Will the Minister indicate whether the Taoiseach, prior to the Government's decision to appoint Mr. O'Flaherty to this post, indicated that Mr. O'Flaherty had questions to answer in order to deliver the "missing bit"? Did the Minister for Finance or the Taoiseach put those questions to Mr. O'Flaherty? Did the Minister discuss with the Taoiseach the meaning of the comments he made last night before deciding to answer a question on behalf of the Taoiseach in respect of the various invitations and suggestions he made to Mr. Hugh O'Flaherty to answer questions in order to provide the 'missing bit' in the Sheedy saga?

MR. McCREEVY:

As Deputy Quinn is undoubtedly aware, discussions and conversations between the Taoiseach and the Minister for Finance are confidential.

MRS. OWEN:

The Minister was sent in here to answer our questions.

MR. QUINN:

Do I understand that, after only three years in office, the Charlie

McCreevy who was revered as being blunt and painstaking is the arrogant man who sits in front of me now? Is it not an indication of the extraordinary transformation that has occurred within the past 36 months that the Minister should state that conversations between himself and the Taoiseach in respect of the appointment of a man the Government wanted to impeach are confidential? Is that the stage we have reached? Is such behaviour worthy of Deputy McCreevy?

AN LEAS-CHEANN COMHAIRLE:

It is not appropriate to question—

MR. MCCREEVY:

If I was to attend a school where lessons in arrogance were taught, I would attend the one frequented by Deputy Quinn.

A DEPUTY:

The Deputy has got under the Minister's skin.

MR. [LOUIS J.] BELTON:

We have returned to the days of the banana republic.

'ONE OF THE BIGGEST CAPITAL PROJECTS EVER CONTEMPLATED IN THE HISTORY OF THE STATE'

The PDs get the jitters about the Bertie Bowl

Progressive Democrat scepticism about the Taoiseach Bertie Ahern's pet project, Stadium and Sports Campus Ireland (popularly, but not correctly, referred to as the Bertie Bowl), never really went away. But rarely had the Coalition partners been so publicly divided on a fundamental issue as here in May 2001.

The Government had just agreed to commission independent consultants to examine the cost of the project but the then Fine Gael leader Michael Noonan claimed Bertie Ahern's 'field of dreams' would need more than £1 billion. 'The Taoiseach, without consultation with his partners in Government or without sanction from the Minister for Finance, is prepared to throw any amount of money at the project to ensure that this monument to his ego is put in place,' he said.

Defending the project, the then Sports Minister Dr. Jim McDaid said the net cost to the Exchequer would be £350 million. He assured the House that the project was not being provided at the expense of hospitals, housing and schools. 'Funding for Sports Campus Ireland poses absolutely no threat to that expenditure,' he said.

PD Bobby Molloy appeared to contradict Dr. McDaid, saying, 'Abbotstown can only proceed by displacing other projects.' He put the tensions within the coalition on display by demanding the PDs must 'know exactly what the Government is being asked to sign up for'.

(01 May 2001)

MR. [BOBBY] MOLLOY: It is well known that the proposed development of Stadium and Sports Campus Ireland at Abbotstown has given rise to concern within my party. The Abbotstown project is large and ambitious by any standards. With the construction industry working at full capacity there is a risk that building costs could soar out of control and we have to guard against that. We must also be conscious of the changed economic circumstances. Our economy is still growing strongly, thanks to the Government's excellent stewardship and the proven success of its policies, but the pace of growth has slackened. The slowdown in the United States and the foot and mouth crisis here have applied the brakes to the Irish economy. We will still grow at more than twice the EU average this year but the need for fiscal prudence is now greater than ever.

Ministers have recently been asked to scale back spending plans in a number of areas. We have been asked to trim capital investment proposals against a background of rising tender prices. As a result we are looking at our priorities to determine where capital investment is needed most, what projects are of immediate importance and what ones can be deferred for a year or two. It is in this context that we have to look at Stadium and Sports Campus Ireland.

This is one of the single biggest capital projects on the drawing board. It is one of the biggest capital projects ever contemplated in the history of the State. It will tie up considerable resources in the construction industry for years. Given the tightness in that industry, Abbotstown can only proceed by displacing other projects. It is vital, therefore, that we get a clear picture of what is involved before proceeding further.

The Progressive Democrats has called for a comprehensive overview of the whole project. Such an overview was agreed between the two Government parties this morning. The terms of reference for that overview have been agreed and work on appointing the consultants will get under way with immediate effect. We want to see the full picture and to know exactly for what the Government is being asked to sign up. Specifically we want to know the full cost of relocating the State laboratories from the lands at Abbotstown, of providing all the necessary infrastructural links to the site, especially road and rail, the construction cost of Stadium Ireland, the main component of the campus and each of the other component projects—

MR. [EMMET] STAGG: The party is a bit late now.

MR. MOLLOY: —the exact level of private sector finance that will be forthcoming by way of public-private partnership arrangements, the total capital cost to the Exchequer of the entire project—

AN CEANN COMHAIRLE [SÉAMUS PATTISON]: The Deputy has less than one minute remaining.

MR. RABBITTE: Do not stop him. It is great stuff.

MR. MOLLOY: —and the ongoing running costs, if any, to be borne by the Exchequer once the stadium and the other facilities have been completed.

Much of this information will flow from the competitive tendering process which is currently under way and due for completion next month. Once we have a full picture of the costs involved we will be able to make a decision. No further legally binding agreements will be entered into until the overview is completed. This is a sensible, reasonable way to proceed and manage the development of a major and complex capital project, the scale of which has never been attempted here. The Progressive Democrats believe this approach represents the best way of protecting the interests of the taxpayer.

There have been several cases in the past where public capital projects have seriously overrun their budgets. Quite rightly, we then have investigations, examinations and inquiries by Oireachtas committees to find out what went wrong—we try to be wise after the event. The Progressive Democrats believe that with this project it is better to be wise before the event and we should make a more accurate and rigorous estimate of the total costs involved before we commit the taxpayers to funding the development.

Re-Elected!

The Coalition is returned to power

When Fianna Fáil and the Progressive Democrats were re-elected in May 2002, it was the first time an outgoing government had been returned since 1969. Fianna Fáil increased their Dáil representation to 81 seats. The PDs doubled their number from four TDs to eight, defying some expectations but presumably not the Tánaiste's (she had placed a bet on this result).

The Opposition parties swallowed their pride and offered their congratulations. The then Labour leader Rúairí Quinn paid tribute to his constituency colleague Michael McDowell who—third time lucky—had 'finally got the timing right and managed to get into Leinster House at the same time as his party gets into Government'. And Tánaiste Mary Harney was quizzed on whether or not she had faith in her coalition partners.

(06 June 2002)

MR. [BRENDAN] HOWLIN: Did the Tánaiste tell the people not to trust Fianna Fáil?

MS. [MARY] HARNEY: I will deal with that in a moment.

MR. G. MITCHELL: What did the Progressive Democrats say about the Romanian dictator?

MS. HARNEY: The people did not see any alternative Government to the one that is being put in place at the moment. On the issue of trust, I say to Deputy Howlin that on no occasion during the course of the general election campaign did I say that the people with whom I have shared Government for the past five years could not be trusted. I did not say that and I do not believe that.

MR. [BRENDAN] HOWLIN: Is the Tánaiste disowning Deputy McDowell already?

MR. [EMMET] STAGG: The Minister said Fianna Fáil could not be trusted.

MS. HARNEY: I was in office with people who are honest and decent and who work hard. I said, and I strongly believe, that the coalition model of Government which has been in operation for some time is the most effective form of Government.

MR. G. MITCHELL: The Progressive Democrats are not in coalition. They are an addendum.

MS. HARNEY: Coalition delivers better checks and balances and scrutinises policies in a more critical fashion than single party Government. That does not apply to any one party but to all parties.

I listened this morning to Deputies talking about centre right and centre left parties. Many Members are not ideologues and we do not take our politics from text books. We did not have to go to university to study political science. When I sat where Deputy Cullen is sitting now the Labour Party sat on my left and Fianna Fáil sat on my right. As the Ceann Comhairle looks down at the House the Labour Party is centre right and Fianna Fáil and the Progressive Democrats are on the left.

MR. STAGG: The Minister's politics are right wing. Where she sits in the House does not matter.

MS. HARNEY: It all depends on one's perspective. Is Tony Blair leading a centre right Government in Britain?

MR. [BERNARD] DURKAN: Yes.

MS. HARNEY: Many of the Labour Party's allies are in Government in several European countries where they implement the kind of policies that have been implemented in this country over the past five years. They do so not for ideological reasons, but because those policies work. Anyone who thinks reducing the burden of tax on working people is right wing needs to think again.

A 'SORDID LITTLE DEAL'

The Taoiseach gets Thursdays 'off'

Cracks appeared in the fledgling 'Alternative Coalition' (consisting of Fine Gael, Labour and possibly the Greens) in October 2003 as Labour prepared to strike a controversial deal with the Government.

This followed the formation of a pragmatic alliance between the Greens, Sinn Féin and some Independents. The Technical Group (mockingly dubbed 'Green Féin') did not share policies but had one more TD than Labour— relegating that party to third place in the pecking order for quizzing the Taoiseach and contributing to debates.

Despite accusations of betrayal from the other Opposition parties, Labour backed a proposal reducing the prominence of the Technical Group and restoring itself as the second-largest opposition force.

Part of the deal was that the time Taoiseach Bertie Ahern had to appear in the chamber was reduced. 'How does that go down with the workers of this country?' demanded Green Party leader Trevor Sargent. It was a 'sordid little deal', according to Sinn Féin's Caoimhghín Ó Caoláin.

(23 October 2002)

MR. [ENDA] KENNY:	Before agreeing to the Order of Business, I would like clarification of reports that the Taoiseach is to absent himself from the House every Thursday.
AN CEANN COMHAIRLE [RORY O'HANLON]:	That does not arise at this stage.
MR. KENNY:	I want clarification on whether we will have an executive Government without any responsibility to the House and the people.
AN CEANN COMHAIRLE:	This proposal deals specifically with statements on Iraq.
MR. KENNY:	We cannot have a situation where the Taoiseach absents himself deliberately when there are questions to be answered.
AN CEANN COMHAIRLE:	Is the Deputy opposed to taking statements on Iraq?
MR. KENNY:	I am if I do not get clarification on these reports. Since I was elected to the House during the period of office of former Taoiseach Liam Cosgrave, every Taoiseach has answered questions on Thursdays.

AN CEANN COMHAIRLE:	I call Deputy Trevor Sargent.
MR. KENNY:	Does the Taoiseach expect to come to the House on Tuesday afternoons and to leave for the rest of the week on Wednesday at 4 o'clock? This is disgraceful carry on.

(Interruptions.)

MR. [BERNARD] ALLEN:	Can we discuss this in the morning or can it be discussed at all?
AN CEANN COMHAIRLE:	It can be discussed at another time but it has nothing to do with Iraq. I call Deputy Trevor Sargent.

(Interruptions.)

MR. [MICHAEL] RING:	It appears that we do not count anymore. There is no respect for this House outside here.
AN CEANN COMHAIRLE:	I have noticed that is the case when Deputies do not keep order in the House.
MR. SARGENT:	We are objecting to the proposal on the basis that this is not just a case of statements about a despot in Iraq. Not unlike Deputy Kenny's point, this is about Ireland deciding whether or

not to take part in a war and the Dáil needs to vote on the matter.

AN CEANN COMHAIRLE:

The proposal is on how we debate the matter rather than its content.

MR. SARGENT:

I object to the fact that it is only statements. We need to vote on the matter and recognise that other despots, like Hitler, tried to remove accountability from parliament and that the Taoiseach is trying to remove accountability from the Dáil and wants a one and a half day week. How does that go down with the workers of the country?

AN CEANN COMHAIRLE:

Deputy Sargent is out of order.

MR. SARGENT:

How does that go down with the workers of this country? He wants a one and a half day week so that he can open pubs in Mostar and Hungary and all around Europe. That is what he is at.

AN CEANN COMHAIRLE:

I ask the Deputy to resume his seat.

MR. [CAOIMHGHÍN] Ó CAOLÁIN:

Will the Taoiseach advise and confirm if this Government has entered into a sordid little deal with the Labour Party in the House in order to allow this Taoiseach absent himself—

AN CEANN COMHAIRLE: That does not arise. We are debating proposals for discussing Iraq.

MR. Ó CAOLÁIN: —from the business of this House on a Thursday? We have here a proposal to allow the Taoiseach a one and a half day week and—

AN CEANN COMHAIRLE: The Deputy is out of order. I ask the Deputy to resume his seat while the Chair is on its feet.

MR. Ó CAOLÁIN: The quid pro quo for this is that the Labour Party will get the numbers—

AN CEANN COMHAIRLE: Does Deputy Ó Caoláin wish to leave the House? I call Deputy Michael Higgins.

MR. STAGG: Make up your numbers with Mr. Lowry.

(Interruptions.)

MR. [CAOIMHGHÍN] Ó CAOLÁIN: The Labour Opposition would let the Taoiseach stay away all the time.

MR. STAGG: I presume the Deputy would like to take over himself.

PART SIX

Parting Shots

ONE LINE WONDERS

'I commend the Taoiseach on his choice of somebody with the sensitive touch of Deputy Cowen to bear responsibility for the children of the nation.'
Pat Rabbitte hails the new Minister for Health and Children.
(26 June 1997)

'. . . when you are from Kerry and as ignorant as us, you have to be fierce clever.'
Dick Spring quotes John B. Keane when stepping down as Labour leader. (06 November 1997)

'He is the quietest Minister for Finance to occupy the office. I searched for statements made by him since he was appointed but it would be as easy to find geraniums in the desert.'
Michael Noonan on, of all people, Charlie McCreevy.
(26 November 1997)

'Men are not a beleaguered species.'
Mary Wallace, the then Junior Justice Minister, rejects Brian Hayes' proposal to establish a commission on the status of men.
(05 February 1998)

'The question of chemical castration must be given serious consideration.'
Beverley Cooper-Flynn suggests a suitable punishment for sex offenders. (07 May 1998)

'It would appear, to put the most charitable interpretation on it, that Mr. Burke was embarrassingly good at political fund-raising and at building up a large personal political war chest.'
The Taoiseach Bertie Ahern responds to revelations about Ray Burke. (03 June 1998)

'Fianna Fáil is up there with the Christian Democrats in Italy and the RPI in Mexico.'
John Gormley claims the Soldiers of Destiny are in the 'top five' of the world's most corrupt political parties during a debate on the Tribunals. (03 June 1998)

'This is the arch blatherer of Dáil Éireann.'
Mary O'Rourke takes on Emmet Stagg during a debate on an ESB dispute. He had just asked her to 'stop substituting blather for real action'. (11 March 1999)

'Women tell me that many of them enjoy snooker and have a particular affinity for studying the backsides of some of the world's famous snooker players.'
Austin Deasy during a debate on legislation to preserve certain sporting events on terrestrial TV. (02 June 1999)

'That is the first time Deputy Higgins has smiled in two and a half years. It is like moonlight on a tombstone.'
John Bruton catches Joe Higgins allowing himself a self-congratulatory grin after his latest witticism (this time at the expense of the Labour Party). (02 November 1999)

'Is the Taoiseach aware the former Taoiseach, Mr. Haughey, had a gingko tree and said if one eats two leaves a day it improves the memory?'
Brendan Howlin concludes that CJH didn't follow his own recommendation. (02 November 1999)

'There was fruit on that tree in North Dublin.'
P.J. Sheehan during a debate on Ansbacher accounts.
(09 February 2000)

'This was the worst team we ever put on the field.'
Michael Ring's assessment of the Eircom flotation squad—Mary O'Rourke, Ray MacSharry and Alfie Kane. (30 May 2000)

'If men gave birth, male medical personnel, male administrators and bureaucrats and male politicians would ensure the whole process of labour and delivery was as pain free and stress free as possible.'
Alan Shatter during a debate on hospital services. (22 June 2000)

'The Taoiseach should send us some pigeons.'
Jim O'Keeffe complains about the delay in equipping new Leinster House offices with modern technology. (03 October 2000)

'There are still people in Ireland who think Mr. Haughey rode in the Tour de France.'
Michael Noonan, in a debate on the Bertie Bowl, observes the tradition of Irish politicans rebranding themselves as sports fanatics for popularity purposes. (01 May 2001)

'A predecessor of mine, former Deputy Gerard Collins, once said that the Labour Party was like Mother Mo Chroí's old dog, it would go halfway down the road with any passer-by.'
John O'Donoghue lashes out at Labour. (01 May 2001)

'. . . when a person thinks he is slightly more than half-right, he must stand up for what he believes and address that matter with whatever tools are available.'
Liam Lawlor explains why he keeps on fighting.
(07 February 2002)

'I am not an uncritical, unthinking, cap-touching admirer of the United States.'
Willie O'Dea's declaration of independence. (30 January 2003)

'The new Government jet was discussed on "Morning Ireland" this morning. Is there a jacuzzi on the jet, how many passengers will it take and will there be mixed bathing?'
Pat Rabbitte's question . . .

'We are not smoked salmon socialists.'
. . . Dermot Ahern's response. (26 February 2003)

'Is the Tánaiste prepared to see Mountjoy Prison become a Fianna Fáil-Progressive Democrats Gulag for hundreds of workers and pensioners over the next few months, because that is what will happen?'
Joe Higgins, unrepentant after his month-long stay in prison for his part in the so-called anti-bin tax campaign. He had defied a High Court injunction prohibiting him from obstructing waste collection. (21 October 2003)

'We are becoming elderly listening to the Deputy.'
Michael Smith to Seán Ryan. (25 February 2004)

'...the air of injured innocence of the most senior people involved might come from a Monty Python script.'
Joe Higgins had just asked if the Minister for Justice intended sending water canons into the boardrooms of top banks to flush out fraud. (01 June 2004)

'I thought the staff in Iveagh House had finessed Deputy Cowen a bit but they obviously have not.'
Pat Rabbitte finds Brian Cowen unchanged after his move from Foreign Affairs to Finance. (05 October 2004)

'I am quite enjoying the fact that the Labour Party has not been so upset for 20 years.'
The Taoiseach Bertie Ahern after Pat Rabbitte said Mr. Ahern had 'come out' as a Socialist. (16 November 2004)

'Perhaps he will get his girlfriend to interview him again on RTÉ3.'
Willie O'Dea later apologised to John Deasy's fiancée, TV3's Maura Derrane, who had interviewed Mr. Deasy and Justice Minister Michael McDowell for a news report. He also apologised to RTÉ for 'implying, by way of a slip of the tongue, that it has the resources to support a third channel'. (26 February 2004)

'I sincerely hope the Army chiefs of staff have already locked up the tanks lest Corporal Willie makes a beeline for the Curragh to play with the new toys the Taoiseach has given him.'
Joe Higgins salutes the new Minister for Defence . . .

'Thank you, Trotsky.'
. . . Willie O'Dea returns the compliment. (09 September 2004)

'I had to negotiate with him in a horizontal position as they might say but there was no jogging involved.'
On his last day in the Dáil, John Bruton recalls negotiating with Bertie Ahern who was confined to bed with a back problem at the time. (27 October 2004)

'St. Patrick's Day has traditionally been on 17 March and I would no more attempt to change that date than change the date of Christmas Day.'
John O'Donoghue rules out a Green Party suggestion that a summertime festival would be more family-friendly and easier to police. (25 May 2004)

'Deputy Higgins should stick with the kebabs.'
Conor Lenihan faced demands to resign as a Junior Minister after
this reference to Turkish GAMA construction workers, on behalf
of whom Joe Higgins had been campaigning. (18 May 2005)

SIEGE AT JADOTVILLE
THE IRISH ARMY'S FORGOTTEN BATTLE

by Declan Power

The Irish soldier has never been a stranger to fighting the enemy with the odds stacked against him. The notion of charging into adversity has been a cherished part of Ireland's military history.

In September 1961 another chapter should have been written into the annals, but it is a tale that lay shrouded in dust for years.

The men of A Company, 35th Irish Infantry Battalion, arrived in the Congo as a UN contingent to help keep the peace. For many it would be their first trip outside their native shores. Some of the troops were teenage boys, their army-issue hobnailed boots still unbroken. They had never heard a shot fired in anger.

A Company found themselves tasked with protecting the European population at Jadotville, a small mining town in the southern Congolese province of Katanga. It fell to them to try try and protect people who later turned on them. On 13 September 1961 the bright morning air of Jadotville was shattered by the sound of automatic gunfire . . .

WELCOME TO HELL

AN IRISHMAN'S FIGHT FOR LIFE INSIDE THE BANGKOK HILTON

by COLIN MARTIN

Written from his cell and smuggled out page by page, Colin Martin's autobiography chronicles an innocent man's struggle to survive inside one of the world's most dangerous prisons.

After being swindled out of a fortune, Martin was let down by the hopelessly corrupt Thai police. Forced to rely upon his own resources, he tracked down the man who conned him and, drawn into a fight, accidentally stabbed and killed that man's bodyguard.

Martin was arrested, denied a fair trial, convicted of murder and thrown into prison—where he remained for eight years.

Honest and often disturbing—but told with a surprising humour—*Welcome to Hell* is the remarkable story of how Martin was denied justice again and again.

In his extraordinary account, he describes the swindle, his arrest and vicious torture by police, the unfair trial, and the eight years of brutality and squalor he was forced to endure.

IF YOU'RE NOT IN BED BY 10, COME HOME

by Martin Bengtsson

Martin Bengtsson's story contains all the ingredients of best-selling fiction—murder, intrigue, sex, royalty, and espionage. And yet it is all true.

Having started out as a bank clerk, he soon made his escape and began smuggling cigarettes for the Mafia along the Mediterranean coastline.

Among many subsequent adventures – some legal, some not so legal – he worked as a bodyguard for a Saudi Arabian prince, partied with Errol Flynn and Gracie Fields, was part of a CIA hit squad and smuggled guns for African rebels.

His story has many threads which are sewn together in a wonderful narrative impossible to replicate.

Bengtsson's voice—witty, debonair and emphatically non-conformist—sings from the pages, whether he is describing his career as a stuntman on Spaghetti Westerns, or revealing his secret life as an MI5 spy.

Looking back, he says he was never motivated by politics or patriotism. 'I can honestly say I did it for the money.'

CINDERELLA MAN

by Michael C. Delisa

**Now the subject of a Major
Motion Picture starring Russell Crowe**

In 1934, in the depths of the Great Depression, a failed boxer with broken hands came off the welfare rolls for one more fight to feed his wife and three children. Four bouts later, one of the bravest men ever to step into a ring was the heavyweight champion of the world, in the greatest comeback in sports history. Jim Braddock became the 'Cinderella Man,' and inspired a troubled nation.

Once he had been a contender, a top light-heavy with skill and guts, until injuries, defeats and the aftershock of the Wall Street Crash left him toiling in railway yards and on New Jersey's Hudson River docks to pay the rent.

But one man never lost faith: his manager, Joe Gould. The tiny, loquacious Jew and the tall, straight-talking Irishman made an odd but inseparable couple, and their belief in each other was unshakable, even when Braddock entered the ring a 10-1 underdog against feared champion Max Baer, who had been blamed for the deaths of two men in the ring. How the family man with a simple cause triumphed over overwhelming odds became the stuff of legend.